Buddhist-Based Universities in the United States

Buddhist-Based Universities in the United States

Searching for a New Model in Higher Education

Tanya Storch

LEXINGTON BOOKS
Lanham • Boulder • New York • London

Published by Lexington Books
An imprint of The Rowman & Littlefield Publishing Group, Inc.
4501 Forbes Boulevard, Suite 200, Lanham, Maryland 20706
www.rowman.com

Unit A, Whitacre Mews, 26-34 Stannary Street, London SE11 4AB

British Library Cataloguing in Publication Information Available

Library of Congress Cataloging-in-Publication Data
The hardback edition of this book was previously catalogued by the Library of Congress as follows:

Storch, Tanya.
Buddhist-based universities in the United States : searching for a new model in higher education /
Tanya Storch.
p. cm.
Includes bibliographical references and index.
1. Buddhist universities and colleges–United States. 2. Education, Higher–Religious aspects–Buddhism. I. Title.
LC929.7.U6S76 2015
378'.070973–dc23
2015004690

ISBN 978-0-7391-8408-0 (cloth : alk. paper)
ISBN 978-1-4985-1706-5 (pbk. : alk. paper)
ISBN 978-0-7391-8409-7 (ebook)

Printed in the United States of America

Contents

Introduction

Buddhist-based, Buddhist-inspired, or simply Buddhist University are synonymous terms which I use in reference to a particular type of institution of higher learning: a university that is state-accredited, which offers degrees in liberal arts and professional fields, and at the same time uses Buddhist pedagogical principles.

The Buddhist universities which I write about in this book are different from institutions specializing in teaching Buddhist philosophy and practice to lay people wishing to develop a Buddhist lifestyle, or monastics wishing to become clergy, for the latter do not offer programs in liberal arts and professional fields. Diamond Mountain University in Arizona, Won Institute of Graduate Studies in Pennsylvania, Institute of Buddhist Studies in Hawaii, or Dhammakaya Open University in California all are good examples of this type of institution. But the Buddhist-based universities which I am interested in are represented by:

1. University of the West, founded on the principles of Taiwanese Buddhism in 1991 by Master Xingyun and located in Rosemead, CA;
2. Dharma Realm Buddhist University, founded on the principles of Chinese Buddhism in 1976 by Master Xuan Hua and located in the City of Ten Thousand Buddhas, CA;
3. Naropa University, founded on the principles of Tibetan Buddhism in 1974 by Lama Chogyam Trungpa and located in Boulder, CO; and
4. Soka University of America, founded on the principles of Japanese Soka Gakkai in 1987 by Mr. Ikeda Daisaku and located in Aliso Viejo, CA.[1]

To begin with, very little is known about these four universities not only by the general public but even in academic circles. Hundreds of books are published annually which discuss philosophy and history of Buddhism, yet most specialists in the history of American Buddhism are unaware that there are four Buddhist-inspired universities in the United States which function with a good degree of success in a present-day troubled economy, and despite many problems befalling American education.[2] They attract students from all segments of the population and are extremely diverse in an ethnical, cultural, and religious sense, enrolling students from nearly forty countries. Buddhist universities are self-sustained, and hundreds of their graduates annually join the national work-force, carrying with them not merely professional skills but a unique perspective on life that favors interconnectedness, mindfulness, and compassion for all living beings.

Buddhist universities are unique because, although other Asian religions, such as Hinduism, Bahaism, Sikhism, Confucianism, and Daoism, enjoy wide cultural-social support, none of the above has created an institution of higher learning comparable to a Buddhist-based university. To further this notion of uniqueness, one must be reminded that the United States has only two Jewish Universities[3] and only one Islamic University[4] which are typologically similar to the Buddhist universities of our study—they, too, offer degrees in professional fields and liberal arts and, at the same time, build the entire educational experience on moral, spiritual, and philosophical principles of their given religions. The Buddhist-based universities must also be recognized as a new global phenomenon because they do not exist in other Western countries known for their religious tolerance and political will to experiment with new forms of education.

Another even more important reason that attracted me to studying Buddhist universities in the United States, is my deep concern (shared by many of my colleagues) about the future of American higher education. I have served as a Professor of Religious Studies at the University of New Mexico, Albuquerque; the University of Pennsylvania, Philadelphia; the University of Florida, Gainesville; and currently at the University of the Pacific, Stockton; and I have observed throughout many years of teaching how students' and faculties' attitudes toward higher education have slowly filled with what must be characterized as cynicism and despair. What is failing higher education today is not merely its cost. According to recent polls conducted by the Pew Research Center, *Time Magazine*, and the Carnegie Corporation, more than 50 percent of American adults think that higher education is in crisis and moving in the wrong direction, at the same time, more than 60 percent of senior higher education administrators express the opinion that their sector of education is in crisis (Budwig, Sandell, Selingo, Arum, and online public forum, "Colleges in Crisis").

Now, compared to this, the educational processes and experiences I had the fortune to observe and study at the Buddhist-based universities must be characterized (and they have been consistently characterized by all people involved in them) as being purposeful, useful in real life, and driven by a mission to improve human character and help communities; in short, these have been characterized by all the people interviewed for the book as *leading in the right direction.*

Studying Buddhist-based universities convinced me that the "right kind" of education is still possible. It will definitely require internal changes at all levels, but it can be done, because the "secret" of the Buddhist universities' success is not in their affiliation with particular spiritual traditions, but in that, by following pedagogical principles developed within these traditions, they established the "right" moral foundation and "right" motivation for providing higher education to their students. In the system they have created, nobody falls through the cracks, and everybody works together, from a custodian to the president, to achieve the commonly shared goals. This type of pedagogy is based on the notions of oneness and interconnectedness, where a university's community is seen as one family. This, of course, does not lead to lowering standards of academic performance, as some may suspect. Contrary to this, students graduating from the Buddhist-inspired universities demonstrate high levels of academic and professional preparedness. For instance, nearly 40 percent of Soka University's graduates went on to graduate programs according to *2008 Peterson's Guide to Four Year College*; this is significantly higher than the national average of barely 20 percent. At the same time, the graduation rate from Buddhist-based universities is close to 90 percent (compared to barely above 50 percent nation-wide); and more than 80 percent of graduates find work in their chosen professions. All of them report that they enjoy a high degree of satisfaction (eight or higher on a ten point scale) from their lives, professions, and especially, from the sense of having purpose to their life and being prepared for its psychological challenges.

This book is meant to initiate a public discussion of education that is offered by Buddhist pedagogy. It seems that, with our higher education being in serious crisis, its positive experiences need to be studied and understood for potential application on other campuses.

NOTES

1. It is most likely that Maitripa College in Portland, OR, which was established in 2006 as a Tibetan Buddhist Theosophical College, will become the fifth Buddhist University in the United States. It is currently affiliated with the Foundation for Preservation of the Mahayana Traditions and is applying for regional accreditation.

2. To the best of my knowledge, there is not a single monograph dedicated to the history of, and educational programs at, American Buddhist universities. The history of the Naropa

University has been studied somewhat better due to the popularity of its founder among the influential social-cultural activists of the '70s and '80s.

3. Yeshiva University was founded in 1886 in New York. Today it combines contemporary academic programs with the moral teachings of the Torah. In 2007, the American Jewish University (AJU) was created as a result of merging the University of Judaism with Brandeis-Bardin College. It offers degrees in bioethics, psychology, liberal arts, business, communication, political science, and Jewish studies.

4. Islamic American University (IAU) in Southfield, Michigan, offers courses in history and spiritual teachings of Islam along with the degrees in Liberal Arts and several professional fields.

Chapter One

University of the West

FIRST ENCOUNTER

For each of the four Buddhist-based universities, I give a description of my first encounter with the university's campus. I'm doing so for two reasons. One is that the first impression of the campus characterizes a college or university more than any other potential information students may receive about the institution they plan to attend (Selingo, 30–33). But my second reason is even more important. In the last decades, our colleges and universities have nearly completely succumbed to a market-model of selling higher education. Campuses have been turned into a primary marketing tool in this process, and they are now attracting students by boasting of the most luxurious environments they can provide, and by promising to satisfy every material desire students may have. Such campuses look more like expensive hotels and upscale resorts than places inviting our young people to study and pursue their moral and intellectual cultivation.[1]

Against this background, visiting the Buddhist-based universities was a real relief and a breath of fresh air. Not a single one of them looked like a resort or expensive hotel, and yet, their architectural and natural beauty was obvious. Even more impressive for me was discovering the dignified and inexpensive ways in which this has been accomplished.

The beauty of these campuses, I dare to say, is consistent with the goals of the Buddhist-based education pursued in the classrooms such as the mindful approach to the environment as well as people spending time with nature, self-reflection and meditation, and cultivation of peaceful and resourceful approaches to problem-solving. These campuses' simple, elegant, and artistic forms remind everyone of the very purpose for being there, which is to provide and receive well-rounded liberal and professional education while pursuing personal growth and cultivation, and to learn about global human interconnectedness and how to be a good member of a large community. All structural, internal, and landscape designs are aligned with these principles, and everything is purposely constructed to hold the ultimate honorable goal: to raise future generations who will not be solely dedicated to making money and satisfying material desires, but who will learn to be conscientious human beings living in harmony with others and with their natural surroundings.

This is why I paid serious attention to each Buddhist campus and learned how it is organized in addition to learning about its history, academic programs, faculty, and students. So, let us now have our first encounter with the University of the West (UWest). When we arrive here, we enter a different world, compared to the busy, polluted, and highly congested districts of Los Angeles. When we begin our walk, there is a sense of having stepped into a place that is very different from the rest of the city not only because the environs are clean and beautiful, but because we are surrounded by an unusual sense of peace and quiet. We can actually hear nature—birds, fountains, and rustling of leaves—because they appear against the background of an ever-present, soothing silence. The sounds of human activities are gentle and conducted with the awareness of the presence of others. Loud sounds of television and music are absent. There are no disruptive noises from the leaf-blowers. Nor do we hear people speaking in loud or angry voices to each other and on their mobile phones. Everyone on this campus is polite and everyone immediately attends to the needs of a stranger (at first, I was shocked by this, and it felt unreal).

The central experience of UWest involves walking on a long road, surrounded on both sides by tall cypress trees. This road goes continuously up, creating a bit of a challenge for someone who is out of shape. It also symbolically represents the challenges people encounter here when they become students, for they will struggle with themselves trying to reach the highest level of consciousness and to fully realize their human potential. Noteworthy, there are three options one can choose from while climbing the road. One can climb all the way up, exercise one's legs, and get plenty of oxygen for the lungs. Or, one can use the elevator from half-way if one is injured, or disabled, or must arrive faster. The third is what I would call the esoteric option. In one place on the road, one can walk between the two cypresses and arrive to the top rather easily. Only those who have stayed on campus long enough know about this third option, which compels me to quote Master Xingyun, the university's founder: "Buildings do not speak, nor do flowers and grass have anything to say, and yet, if you listen ever so carefully, you will hear the Dharma being spoken everywhere" (Fu, 123).

I chose to walk all the way up to the top and needed a few minutes to catch my breath. Then, I turned to the left, toward the edge of the cliff, and came across a small wooden structure painted white. It stands by itself on the edge of the cliff. It is a Meditation Pavilion. Because of its location right on the edge of the cliff, one can see the distant dark-blue mountains on the horizon. But when one sits down in meditation, one sees the district with cars, shops, and restaurants underneath the feet. The pavilion is built in a traditional Chinese style. Sitting there, with the sounds of chimes and the lotus symbol suspended from the ceiling, brings such a palpable sense of calm and peace—gifts so precious and so difficult to find in our fast-paced and anxiety-filled world.

When other people walked by the Meditation Pavilion, they stopped talking, or if they had to carry on with a conversation, they walked some distance away from it. Every time I sat in that wooden pavilion on the edge of the cliff, I felt peace. My wish is for every American campus to have a place like this—a place where human consciousness can rest and all the worries of the world stop for just a few minutes. Creating such a place on every campus would take a small administrative effort and tiny financial investment, but it would give so much to the students.

Not far from the Meditation Pavilion, there is the "dining hall" with an open deck that overlooks the mountains and is covered by tree branches. One can eat indoors or under the open sky. Eating in the dining hall, three meals a day, is very inexpensive, especially compared to other universities. Food tastes good because the ingredients are purchased from local producers. Help from a local community, and the university's community itself, is often donated to the kitchen.[2]

Our encounter with UWest will not be complete without mentioning that one meets here real Buddhist nuns and monks who participate in the campus's life on par with all other students.[3] These monastics come from more than thirty different countries and, while they could have pursued their education in the institutions specifically designed for the Buddhist clergy, their choice of UWest is made for a purpose—to live and learn in the same environment in which regular American students live and learn. Not all Buddhist-based universities have nuns and monks present on their campuses; and when they do, not all campuses provide for a regular communication between the secular and monastic students as in UWest.

LIFE OF MASTER XINGYUN, FOUNDER OF THE UNIVERSITY OF THE WEST

As already mentioned, the University of the West was founded in 1991 by Master Xingyun.[4] Xingyun represents Taiwanese Foguangshan (Buddha's Light Mountain)[5] monastic order and Humanistic Buddhist traditions (Chandler, 28–78). His most full biography in English appeared in 2008 as a translation from Chinese (Fu) made by Robert Smitheram under the title *Bright Star, Luminous Cloud: The Life of a Simple Monk*. According to this biography, Xingyun was born in 1927 in a small town of Jiangdu in Jiangsu province. His secular name (that was changed when he accepted monastic vows) was Guoshen. His father supported the family by going from place to place operating a small business, and his mother was a typical housewife of that time who shouldered all the responsibilities for the household and cared for the children (Fu, 15).

Because Xingyun was born the second son, his mother lovingly nicknamed him "Second Lord." Besides him, she had three more children, and every one of them appeared to be normal, except for Guoshen. Unusual signs, according to his mother's witness, were seen from his birth. He had one strange birthmark in particular: one side of his face was bright red, while the other was pale, and in the middle of his upper lip, there were two bright red lines. Because of these signs, his mother did not allow him to go out until he was three years old and the marks had nearly disappeared. She also remembered him as a hardworking child who did chores on his own; for instance, he would sweep the living quarters, pick up old leaves from the gutters, and clean ashes from the stove. In the morning, he always went out with a bamboo basket to collect cow manure from the roads.[6]

His sister remembered him as being different from other children for he never quarreled or fought with others. She remembered how, at age three when he could not carry a candy-jar, he dragged it out of the door and invited children to have candy. People were laughing at her and their whole family for raising such a "foolish" child.

Other family members have stories about Xingyun's compassion toward animals. For example, he often found an excuse to walk out into the court-yard with his soup-bowl to feed the dogs. As this was the time of war and people were starving, giving people's food to dogs was not welcomed. But when adults punished him for that, Guoshen said, "Hunger is more painful for dogs than humans because dogs cannot complain." Once he saved a small pigeon and nursed it back to life. When the pigeon flew away, he jumped into the river from sadness (Fu, 17–18).[7]

Whether these are real stories or merely legends created about a Buddhist teacher who has become a symbol of love and compassion for millions of people is just hard to say. It is not unusual for great spiritual leaders, like Mother Teresa or Nelson Mandela, to show signs of moral uprightness rather early in their character development. In the end, I leave the question of these stories' historical reliability to the discretion of the reader.

Xingyun was exposed to Buddhist devotion early in his life. His maternal grandmother was a vegetarian from a young age and she chanted the entire text of *Diamond Sutra*[8] every day of her life, although she was an illiterate woman and could not read the text. His mother received some education and taught him how to read and write. Love and affection between Xingyun and his mother became a very special story in both of their lives. Xingyun was her special son, and she had chosen him to accompany her on a search for her disappeared husband Xingyun's father. Travelling the road to Nanjing in hopes of finding her husband coincided with one of the most turbulent moments in Chinese modern history. The Japanese occupation brought many atrocities of war, and the most violent and bloody of them were happening right in the area through which they were travelling.[9] During this journey with his mother, the 12-year-old Xingyun watched the troops marching toward Nanjing, and it was then that a senior monk from the nearby monastery appeared in front of him and asked whether he would like to join the order of monks. And Xingyun immediately answered, "Yes." But his mother was saddened by her son's decision to seek the Buddha instead of seeking his father. And this is why, despite having already made a decision to become a monk, he continued serving his mother in full accordance with the Chinese-Confucian family ethics.

His commitment to his mother constantly showed in his life. After he had escaped the civil war in mainland China and arrived in Taiwan, he continued seeking for her until he was able to meet her. Finally, he arranged for her to come to the United States and stay at the Hsi Lai Temple—the temple that he himself founded in Southern California. The entire time that his mother was absent from his life and he had no news of her, he stubbornly refused to celebrate his birthdays. Only after he had learned that she was alive and he would be able to see her again (around his sixtieth birthday), did he agree to have a Dharma service in which one thousand people, all of whom had just turned sixty, participated. On that day, he gave a sermon in which he suggested that "all parents in the world are our parents." His mother died in 1996 in California while he was away in Taiwan. He came to the United States immediately, cremated her, and buried her ashes in the Rose Hill Memorial Buddhist Complex near Los Angeles. Then he wrote these words:

> Amid the sounds of those assembled there, chanting scriptures and reciting the Amitabha Buddha's name, I lightly pressed the green button. With a burst of fire, a puff of wind, and a flash of light, I bid eternal farewell to my mother. . . . My mother was twenty-five when she gave birth to my body, and now, seventy years later, I have seen to the cremation of her body. Mother was like a ship that slowly carried me into this human world, while I am like a space shuttle that carries her instantaneously to another realm in space and time . . . I think to myself quietly, between this mundane world and the Pure Land of Ultimate Bliss, that there remains the unchanging bond between mother and son. (Fu, 27)

Going back to his life as a teenager in war-torn China in the late 1930s, he finally received his mother's permission to join the monastery. Life in the monastery was full of challenges which modern Americans cannot even imagine. I purposely give some details here because this would be useful for our students who complain that material difficulties stand in their way to intellectual and moral cultivation and are too difficult to overcome. For instance, Xingyun was not able to send a letter to his mother for a whole year because he was unable to save enough money to pay for one postal stamp. He had to pick through the robes and socks of the monks who had recently died in order to collect things to wear. Because he had to use what was left from other monks, he never had matching socks. His shoes had many holes, and the soles were so worn that he used old cardboard to enhance them.[10]

In the living quarters for the monks, one hundred and ten of them slept in a single dormitory on one long bed. They all slept shoulder to shoulder, and even a simple act of turning to another side was a problem. In the morning, several people washed themselves from one bucket of cold water. And of course, monks in the monastery were perpetually hungry because the gruel served for breakfast was as thin as water, and cooked rice was served only twice a month.

Xingyun spent six years in that monastery. Luckily for him, and also due to his training and personal discipline, he was selected to enter the Jiaoshan Buddhist College in 1945. There, he encountered talented teachers who educated him in literature, geography, history, and biology. No doubt, it was this experience that many years later manifested itself in his commitment to building schools, colleges, and universities, where learning sciences and liberal arts was accompanied by Buddhist practices of character-building and community-service.

Having completed his study at the Jiaoshan Buddhist College, he studied further in several monasteries in which he received a thorough education in Vinaya (Buddhist monastic discipline), Tripitaka-scriptures,[11] and Chan meditation. All the while, he knew that he was preparing himself to serve suffering human beings. He wrote: "What most people heard were the volleys of gunfire and the hail of bullets, but what I heard were the cries for help coming from all suffering beings; what most people saw were the corpses strewn about the countryside, but what I saw . . . was the fate of Buddhism hanging in the future's balance" (Fu, 44).

Xingyun had every reason to worry about the future of Buddhism in China because after the Chinese Republic was established in 1912, Western education began taking over, and many intellectuals voted for the downfall of Buddhism. On a practical level, the new government began destroying temples and converting them to schools. A Christian general, Feng Yuxiang (1882–1948), ordered the elimination of Buddhism in Henan region, while killing and expelling hundreds of monks in that area. In Zhejiang province, the government adopted similar policies, but instead of killing, they expelled monks and nuns and confiscated temples for public use.

Amidst this difficult situation, there rose Master Taixu (1889–1947), who proposed a "revolution" in the Buddhist organization with respect to its property management and monastic life-style. In particular, he proposed that monastic communities be re-organized and monks and nuns re-trained to serve people outside the monastery and function as communal teachers, nurses, and social workers. He advocated a new philosophy that monastics should no longer be mired in a fatalistic perspective on life as if it was endless suffering. He began teaching self-sufficiency through one's own labor and moral conduct, and he placed a new emphasis on the fulfilled life-style that can be acquired through tireless services to all living beings.

Although this new vision of Master Taixu was never implemented in a specific Buddhist organization, it deeply impacted Xingyun, who was present during these early experiments. Meanwhile, in China, a military conflict between the Nationalist and Communist forces was turning into a brutal bloodshed. Taixu passed away, and Xingyun was ordered to return to his

lineage seat. He moved to the Dajue Temple and served there until he was
appointed Principal of the Baita Primary School. Having received this appointment, he began developing a new program for the school, but the chaos
of the time made it impossible and he was forced to return to Nanjing. In
1949, the civil war took another dangerous turn, and some monks began
forming relief-teams to provide care for the injured and dead. One of Xingyun's classmates called on six hundred monks to organize a relief-team and
go to Taiwan to provide medical and psychological care for the thousands of
refugees who had recently escaped from mainland China and found a new
home on that island. Xingyun was made a team leader.

He arrived in Taiwan without any luggage. His only long robe was given
to a monk who had suffered from cold on the boat. Due to the calamities of
the journey, out of six hundred, only forty people remained on his team.[12]
The residential Taiwanese were suspicious of the newcomers. Xingyun could
not find a monastery or even a place to spend the night. Once, he slept under
a monastery bell, completely soaked by rain, and when a monk offered him
rice in the morning, his hands shook so hard that he could not receive the
bowl. After several months of such misery he was finally accepted into
Yuanguang Temple in Chungli.

There, he found time and energy to study local dialect. He learned it so
well that when the Abbot gave Dharma-talks, he always asked Xingyun to
serve as an interpreter. Senior monks began taking him outside and allowing
him to participate in religious services which usually earned cash and generous donations of other kinds. However, it was exactly at that moment that
Xingyun realized he must leave that monastery in Chungli to avoid moral
corruption. He allowed himself only one "small corruption": when he was
paid his first $20 for the service, he bought pen, ink, and paper.[13] Soon he
began composing scripts and stories for the youth-radio and publishing his
first Buddhism-influenced spiritual poems. He was published in several mag-
azines: *Free Youth*, *Kan Zhan Daily*, and *Jue-Sheng Monthly*, and nicknamed the "Star of the Buddhist Literary Art."[14]

Despite this success, teaching and preaching Buddhism in Taiwan remained a daunting task. During the Japanese occupation, Taiwanese Buddhism fell under the influence of Japanese traditions which were less strict
than Chinese in terms of monastic discipline. Many senior monks in Taiwan
stopped maintaining necessary rules and allowed themselves to take wives.
Re-establishing monastic discipline was difficult and it caused conflicts and
mutual accusations between the older and younger generations of Chinese
monks. Religious hardships were accompanied by material poverty of the
Taiwanese, who had only recently returned to some social normalcy. Many
of them wished nothing more than simple material satisfaction from life.
Self-discipline and self-sacrifice, preached by Xingyun, had little attraction
for them. Besides, the educational level of most monks was low; they could

only chant the required scripture at the funeral service, but could no longer engage in life-long learning of Buddhist philosophy, literature, and practice. Taiwan's involvement with the United States brought many American Protestants to the capital, and American Christianity began to represent material success and prosperity for thousands of struggling Chinese on the island. For example, Chiang Kai-shek and his wife became devout Christians, as did dozens of other prominent politicians and businessmen.

The ongoing conflict with the People's Republic of China forced the Taiwanese government to continue viewing with suspicion people who had recently arrived from the continent. The mainland monks were regularly imprisoned and interrogated as they were suspected of being "Communist spies." Xingyun was imprisoned twice during his first years in Taiwan.[15] Amidst these uneasy conditions, his life took a dramatic turn for the better when he was invited to preach in Yilan.

Yilan was an under-developed rural place. All Dharma-teachers invited before him had given up and moved out. The monastery was so poor that Xingyun had to sleep under the altar. Eventually, local people cleared out a small windowless room beside the main hall, and this became Xingyun's residence for many years. In Foguangshan museum,[16] I saw some real objects of that time—a broken bamboo bed and sewing machine, which served Xingyun as furniture. When he finally added a chair to these two objects, he was overjoyed. Recalling this after many years he wrote, "When I picked up that chair discarded from the prison . . . I was overjoyed. From then on, every night after everyone had gone to bed, I would drag the electric light hung in front of the Buddha image over to the door of my quarters, where I could read and write with the sewing machine serving as my desk. No amount of waving could dispel the mosquitoes that would buzz around, keeping me company until dawn" (Fu, 66).

In Yilan, Xingyun proved that he was not merely a devoted and self-sacrificing Buddhist, but a brilliant missionary strategist. Within a few years, he built a vibrant community in that area by following three simple steps: 1) he organized a Recitation Center at the monastery where people began to gather on a regular basis to chant together the name of the Buddha Amitabha, and this allowed everyone to participate, even those who were completely illiterate; 2) he engaged young people with love for singing and making new friends, and eventually, established the first Buddhist Youth Choir in history;[17] and 3) he transformed the very idea of a Buddhist missionary and harnessed the enthusiasm of his followers most of whom were young people; he used bicycles to travel from village to village and deliver speeches of compassion, while teaching vegetarianism via cheerful messages of communal singing and story-telling.

Yilan became the center where a completely new form of Buddhism was born—a form that had never before existed and is now known as "Humanistic Buddhism."[18] In 1967, to provide a bigger space for this organization, Xingyun established the Foguangshan (Buddha's Light Mountain) Monastery and Education Center on land purchased by a donor near the city of Kaohsiung in the southwestern part of the island. This ushered in a worldwide Buddhist ecumenical movement. Xingyun knew he was advocating an entirely new approach to how the Buddhist Dharma was to be spread in the modern world. He wrote: "From its beginnings, Buddhism was a religion that focused on the human condition. . . . This is why it had to be "modernized" in each and every age" (Master Xingyun 2006, 35).

Five points, according to him, characterized the "modernized" Buddhism: 1) It must be rational, but not heretical; 2) It must be practical, and not imaginary; 3) It is for this world, and not for another world; 4) It adheres to Buddhism's historical truth, but not to its superstitions; and 5) It is progressive, and not conservative. This type of Buddhism embraced traditional religious ideals, but also, culture and education; and was designed for both monastics and lay people. Culture and education included studying languages, publishing scriptures and dictionaries, opening museums of Buddhist art, holding musical concerts, and creating free libraries and universities around Taiwan and around the world.[19]

Xingyun's form of Buddhism was eventually embraced by Taiwan's government, with President Jiang Jingguo paying visits to the Foguangshan Headquarters, and Xingyun conducting a ceremony for the preservation of the nation in the Sun Yat-sen's Memorial Hall in 1978. The following year, the first Buddhist program was televised nationally, and the first Buddhist summer-camp for children was opened. In the following decades, the influence of the Humanistic Buddhism reached the highest level of international acclaim. In 1984, Xingyun met with the Dalai Lama and established an international mobile clinic offering free medical care. In 1985, he served as the Executive Officer of the Chinese-Tibetan Cultural Association. The same year, "Platform Sutra of the Sixth Patriarch" and "Venerable Master Xingyun Lecture Series" were televised internationally. In 1988, he inaugurated the Hsi Lai Temple in Los Angeles, California; and in 1990, he was invited to attend the inauguration of President George H. W. Bush.

Soon after that, he presided over the "Triple Gem Refuge" ceremony[20] in Kuala Lumpur, Malaysia, which was attended by 80,000 people; and held the "Religious Dialogue of the Century" with Pope John Paul in the Vatican. In 1998, he presided over the first combined Theravada, Mahayana, and Vajrayana Triple Platform Ordination[21] in Bodhgaya, India. In 2001, he arrived at Ground Zero to offer prayers for the victims of the attack on September 11.

He was authorized by the government of the People's Republic of China to escort the Buddha's tooth relic from the Famen Temple in Xi'an to Taiwan. This transfer of, reputedly, the most important Buddhist relic ever known in China, began the process of building the Buddha Memorial Center

ch was completed in December of 2011. One hundred
now the largest existing architectural complex built to
ldha's presence on earth (Xuan, 20–26).
s still alive and active, although his health is rapidly

INSTITUTIONAL HISTORY AND ACADEMIC
PROGRAMS OF THE UNIVERSITY OF THE WEST

The early phase of UWest history is closely linked with the Hsi Lai Temple
inaugurated in 1988 and located in Hacienda Heights albeit in a different
location than the university's campus.[22] The temple is affiliated with the
Foguangshan Buddhist Order of Taiwan and international movement known
as Humanistic Buddhism both of which spread widely around the world due
to the efforts of Xingyun and his followers (Hsing 2006a, 2006b, and 2008).

Although today the Foguangshan and Humanistic Buddhism are rather
popular, drawing millions of supporters in Asia and Western countries alike,
in the eighties, the idea of a large Buddhist temple built in one of the Los
Angeles suburbs did not seem appealing; in fact, it was met with open hostil-
ity from local residents. Irene Lin explained that, as soon as the building of
the Chinese Buddhist temple was announced, multiple cultural, social, and
political problems arose, seriously inhibiting the progress of its construction
(Lin, 383–408). The most notable obstructions stemmed from sentiments
nearly impossible to imagine today, such as strong resentment to the "nuns
wearing their monastic robes," and "having their heads completely shaven."
When a legal opposition was filed, the most prevalent argument was that the
"temple was going to disrupt peace in the neighborhood" and "instigate
violence against the white-American community."

Because of the obstacles, it took nearly twenty years to finish construction
of Hsi Lai Temple. (Newton). In its present form, it is a spectacular architectural complex more than twenty acres in size executed in a traditional Chinese style. The Temple's architecture is designed after the Ming
(1368–1644) and Qing (1644–1911) dynasties' fashion. It includes a massive
gateway, Bodhisattva Hall, Arhats Garden, Avalokiteshvara Garden, court-
yard, Main Shrine, and the dining hall, in which strictly vegetarian food is
served to visitors and monastics in residence.

It is important to understand that, from the beginning, this temple was
designated to serve educational purposes in addition to being a place for
worship and meditation. To attract bigger audiences, a large conference room
was built on one side of the Main Shrine and a large auditorium on the other.
Both conference room and auditorium are equipped with modern technology
and can be used for lectures, discussions, and inter-religious dialogues. On

the level below the Main Shrine, there is the Art Gallery containing rare and precious artifacts from around the world. Adjacent to it is a book store. Offices of the International Translation Center and Buddha's Light Publishing Company are located opposite the Memorial Pagoda behind the Main Shrine.

Consistent with Xingyun's vision of Humanistic Buddhism, the Hsi Lai Temple's programs have been, and still are, dedicated to education and social assistance which are provided to both Asian and European Americans. These include but are not limited to free classes in meditation, Chinese language, and Asian culture. At the same time, Asian immigrants receive social help here, if needed. While some educational programs that originated at the Hsi Lai Temple have been discontinued as they have now become a part of the UWest curriculum, the temple continues to be a place for education and not just worship. It still offers classes in English, Chinese, and Cantonese languages, Buddhist philosophy, history, meditation, yoga, and the arts. It also provides a system of retreats, such as Eight Precepts Retreat and Short-term Monastic Retreat during which participants learn about Buddhist ethics and scriptures and are introduced to practices of vegetarianism, meditation, self-care, and community-involvement. Choirs and a Youth Symphony Orchestra affiliated with the temple offer free music education. After-school programs teach state-approved curricula while employing Buddhist-based pedagogical principles.

Because UWest was founded as a continuation and expansion of some of the programs originally taught at the temple, initially it bore the same name as the temple—Hsi Lai University. An official separation took place in 1991, and in 2006, UWest was accredited by the Western Association of Schools and Colleges (WASC). It is currently organized under the Nonprofit Public Benefit Corporation Law of the State of California. UWest defines itself as a private, nonprofit, nonsectarian, co-educational institution, offering undergraduate, graduate, certificate, and continuing educational programs, whose mission is consistent with the educational mission of California institutions of higher learning.

Although it was Xingyun's idea to found a Buddhist-based University in Southern California, it was definitely due to the heroic efforts of two Buddhologists, Dr. Lewis Lancaster and Dr. Ananda Guruge, that UWest has successfully developed its professional and academic programs and received the WASC accreditation. In the spring of 2014, I interviewed Dr. Lancaster (who was the university's second president) and asked him about memorable moments in the early history of UWest. He told me that Dr. Guruge had prepared all the paperwork required for the WASC accreditation and that when the two of them stood in front of the officials in Oakland with several boxes of documents at their feet, one of the officers confronted them, asking: "Do you think you can really do this?" (Meaning—Do you really think you can start a Buddhist-based university in Los Angeles?) To this, Dr. Lancaster answered affirmatively: "If we couldn't do it, do you think we would be investing our time in it?!" Their strong conviction was based on the knowledge that such a university was not only timely, but also very much needed for the development of a new, embracing East-West model of education.

Dr. Lancaster explained specific functions the Buddhist monastics were to play in the formation of this university by saying, "If monastics wished to have a pure religious experience, they did not have to come to UWest. There are many institutions around the world where they could learn proper monastic rules and have a more traditional Buddhist experience. What made it different for them at our university was that they were receiving training in how to communicate Buddhist philosophy and ethics to modern Americans. Not only were monastics helping students understand Buddhism better, assisting with meditations and ethical principles, but students have become teachers to the monastics, helping them understand modern society with all its problems. Students often expanded cultural-historical horizons of nuns and monks, who had lived for many years in the secluded monastic communities. In short, UWest is not a monastery-like training for students or monastics. Nuns, who came to work here, soon realized they needed lessons in business management to keep the university running. It was from this real necessity that Buddhist Management program was created."

Between 1991 and the present, the university has been under the leadership of seven presidents, including Master Xingyun, Dr. Naichen Chen, Dr. Lewis Lancaster, Dr. Roger Schmidt, Dr. Allen Huang, Dr. C. F. Lee, and Dr. Chin-Shun Wu. Its current president is Dr. Stephen Morgan.

According to the university's website, its two main institutional goals are: 1) to provide a "whole person" education in the context informed by Buddhist wisdom and values, and 2) to facilitate cultural understanding and appreciation between East and West. It expects the following learning outcomes from its students:

1. *Wisdom and Skillful Means*: Students are thoroughly prepared for academic and professional success, and this includes: a) Knowledge: Knowledge of the subject matter and best practices within their field of study; b) Praxis: Ability to integrate theory and practice in their field of study; c) Ethics: Ability to apply professional ethics throughout their career; d) Critical Thinking: Ability to evaluate new information and question underlying assumptions; and e) Communication: Ability to communicate ideas in speech, writing, and other forms of expression.

2. *Self-awareness*: Students are prepared to engage in an on-going process of self-awareness that enables them to lead happy, purposeful lives characterized by healthy relationships with self and others. This

includes a) Balance: Skills for creating balance of body, spirit, and mind; b) Character: Ability to question their attachments, cultivate open-mindedness, and maintain patience and perseverance in the face of on-going change; c) Expression: Abilities for self-expression through work, art, and spiritual practice; and d) Relationship: Abilities that enable them to learn from and in relationship with others and to cultivate respect, compassion, and honesty.

3. *Liberation*: Students recognize the diversity and dignity of all beings and understand the role in the pursuit of social justice. This includes: a) Pluralism: Appreciation of cultural diversity that enables them to thrive in a pluralistic world; b) Environmental justice: Recognition of the value of the natural environment and its impact on social and economic justice; and c) Liberation from suffering: Understanding of how social, economic, and environmental justice lead to the liberation from suffering of all beings.

4. *Interdependence*: Students possess a holistic understanding of global interdependence in order to cultivate compassionate thought, speech, and action in service to themselves, others, and the environment. This includes: a) Service: Ability to take service-oriented approaches to promote and create paths to peace-making, respect, and loving-kindness; and b) Culture: Understanding of how a broad appreciation of human endeavors, such as art, science, and humanities, contributes to social and personal well-being.

When the university opened in 1991, it offered degrees in religious studies, language, psychology, and business. At present, it offers bachelor's degrees in business administration, accounting, computer information systems, international business marketing, psychology, and English; master's degrees in computer information systems, finance, international business, psychology, non-profit organization management, and religious studies; and an executive master of business administration or master of divinity.

Business administration and international business are prominent programs at UWest. Prof. Bill Chen, former chair of the business administration department, was interviewed for this book in 2010. He described what might be called a Buddhist approach to teaching business administration by saying, "Philosophy of Interconnectedness is actually beneficial for business. All our students learn that, in order to be successful in business, one must work toward the enrichment of the entire community. Our students created a group called 'Volunteers for Income Tax Assistance,' VITA. Through the VITA, they helped local people and businesses prepare tax returns. In 2010, 350 local people and businesses participated in this program. This help given to the community allowed our students to have direct experience with real people's financial situations and learn about real businesses' management

problems. They have learned valuable lessons from their successes and fail-
ures and, sometimes, were able to change the situation for the better. Students worked in VITA from early January to mid-April; this group was so
successful that it received the 'Outstanding Service Reward' from IRS. Students also learn about money and business management by helping local
communities through 'Business Assistance Center' registered with local
Chamber of Commerce. Since the earliest stage of their education, students
are trained to work for the better of the local communities, not just to line up
their pockets with profits."[23]

Business administration programs include majors in accounting, international business, marketing, and computer information systems. Graduates
leave the university equipped with the intellectual tools for assuming responsible positions in corporate and not-for-profit organizations. The rate of graduation from business administration programs is high, above 90 percent.
About half of the graduates find jobs within one or two years of graduation,
while others enter graduate programs at other universities.

Another distinguished program at UWest is the Master of Divinity and
Buddhist Chaplaincy. The program, founded by Prof. Danny Fisher, is designed to educate and train chaplains to meet the requirements of the Association of Professional Chaplains. After students become certified, they serve
as chaplains in hospitals, prisons, universities, U.S. military, and other
places. The program offers classes in different Buddhist traditions, as well as
all major religions, and it requires classes in meditation and spiritual counseling, and clinical training.

Prof. Fisher was interviewed for this book in 2013. This is what he said
about the Buddhist Chaplaincy program and Buddhist-inspired education, in
general:

> The student body at UWest, especially, in the Chaplaincy program, is extreme-
> ly diverse. In my classes, I often do not find two students who would share the
> same religious background or even the same Buddhist tradition. At UWest, we
> provide real ethical care for the students. University, overall, functions more
> like a family than an institution. What I mean by this is that no one is allowed
> to "fall through the cracks." When someone is in need, real practical help is
> always provided. One of the most recent events, the death of one of our
> professors, showed us, yet again, how truly interconnected we are. Students,
> faculty, stuff, and administration—all helped this person during his illness, and
> they continued helping his family after his death.

Speaking about not letting people to fall through the cracks, UWest established several fellowships to help students in need, such as UWest Fellowship, Students Life Fellowship, President's and Dean's scholarships; and just
recently established the Lotus Scholarship, which is specifically designed to
support local low-income people. Donations to the Lotus Scholarship were

most generous because local donors knew and appreciated the role UWest plays in local communities.[24]

In discussing learning outcomes pursued at UWest, Fisher underscored two: *Learning to Live Like a Community* and *Learning to be Generous with Others*. He added that these values are rarely taught and learned at other universities, and yet without them, it is impossible to have a truly prosperous democratic society. According to him, all professors at UWest are generous toward their students, and students learn from them what it means to be generous toward others by sharing time, resources, and information. He added that he himself earned a doctoral degree at UWest without paying a single dollar. This is because administration and faculty had known about his tight financial situation and they were generous in providing necessary means to support the education he needed.

> Learning how to live like a community is a core value in Buddhism. In Mahayana, a Bodhisattva takes a special vow which postpones individual achievement of Nirvana for the sake of helping other sentient beings. Many of our students and professors take the Bodhisattva vow very seriously. It must be understood that commitment to helping others is not all about money. Often times, support that is necessary for thriving in higher education can be given in a form of free meals, inexpensive housing, and study-groups which support and enhance progress in difficult academic areas. These forms of humane assistance do not require huge budgets, only the right state of consciousness, and they go a long way to support and motivate our students and help them graduate, so that they can go on to serve the human community outside the university.

Prof. Guruge, one of the founding fathers of UWest, insists that the true value of education must be in teaching the whole person and not just training people in certain technical skills, so that they receive their professional licenses and start making money. I remember him saying that, "To educate our young people so that they become wholesome and ethical and learn what it truly means to be a member of a human community is what our nation needs more than anything. Buddhist-inspired education teaches young people how to be relevant to other people's lives, no matter what area of professional engagement they have chosen. It teaches a peaceful, non-violent approach to solving problems of human existence, and this is the only way to end human conflicts and terrible wars in which we are engaged in today."

In my own university, University of the Pacific in Northern California, I teach a course that covers the history of Buddhist communities in the West. One of the assignments I give to my students requires that they interview professors serving at the Buddhist-based universities. One student interviewed Prof. Darui Long who teaches in the Religious Studies department at UWest. Prof. Long told my student that, for him, the most important Buddhist value is Compassion. Born and raised in China, he had suffered a great deal under the oppressive communist regime. He emphasized that it is necessary to be selfless and care for those who are suffering. "As teachers," he said, "we must be sympathetic toward others, including our colleagues and students. We are all interconnected and experience similar forms of suffering."

Prof. Chu, who teaches classes in meditation, was interviewed by my other student. Chu identified himself as a believer in Buddhism since his early years. He said that he is using Buddhist methods of analysis every day in order to identify causes of his mental anguish. For him, "Awareness" is the most important concept in education because, he said, "When we become aware of our true intentions and consequences of our own actions, we better understand how to help others."

My students concluded that UWest education is successful because it emphasizes Awareness and Compassion. They wrote: "By practicing Compassion and Awareness, the necessary social changes can be created. Through Awareness, we can learn how to work together and help one another. Through Compassion, we reach out to those who need help. No matter what professional field we have chosen, we will have to deal with people who suffer one way or another. If everyone had Awareness and Compassion, many of our social problems could be solved."

Although UWest is now entirely independent from the Hsi Lai Temple, it keeps its historical and professional links to it. This provides faculty and students with unique opportunities to use experiential methods in teaching and learning. The Hsi Lai Temple, with its busy economy and rich daily schedule of activities, as well as with its affiliated charitable organizations in Los Angeles and around the world, creates multiple opportunities for learning practical skills of an accountant, dietician, meditation-instructor, business manager, and so on. It becomes a real educational partner for the university, creating numerous opportunities for internships and jobs for the graduates.

Memorial Complex in Rose Hills, Los Angeles, CA, is one such example. It offers an opportunity to build practical skills for the students majoring in Psychology and Chaplaincy. In general, this complex provides services for the deceased with funeral and memorial rituals and counseling happening every day (I.B.P.S., 28–29). It hosts special spring and fall ceremonies during which large-scale Dharma services are offered. At the same time, it is a modern facility equipped with high-tech and requiring professional management as the computer commands and records must be constantly updated. Intricate artistic architectural designs of the main stupa and private burial chambers must be managed and renovated year around. Given the amount of work necessary for keeping this charitable place in order, students are welcomed to volunteer. Students in Psychology and Chaplaincy Programs stand to learn, first-hand, how to deal with human grief and provide support for the families who have lost their loved ones.

Dr. Venerable Jue Ji, who at the time, served as the Coordinator of Student Life, explained the role the Hsi Lai Temple plays in students' education. Paraphrasing her statements, this is what she said:

1. Students are invited to participate in all religious and spiritual activities conducted at the temple, although this is neither required, nor expected of them.
2. Students have a chance to participate in meditation classes conducted at the temple. They can also volunteer to clean meditation rooms and other public spaces in the temple. They can learn how to cook at the kitchen or volunteer their time as decorators during communal celebrations, international conferences, and business meetings.
3. Students are invited to participate in translation projects where they have a chance to acquire and practice their knowledge of Vietnamese, Chinese, Korean, Spanish, and English languages.
4. The Interfaith programs exist both at the temple and at the university. Students can practice their skills by making presentations to various religious groups congregating at the temple; they can also gain practical knowledge about other religions' practices and beliefs.
5. Students with artistic abilities and love for the arts can volunteer at the Art Museum affiliated with the Temple.
6. Students who plan to work in education can volunteer in the kindergarten and elementary school affiliated with the Temple, as well as in the temple library.

She summarized the benefits of the temple and university working together for the education of young people by concluding: "Temple gives students an extension into real-life with all its opportunities and challenges." She underscored that mingling between monastics and students teaches them about the seriousness of Buddhism: "As students observe nuns and monks, who have dedicated their lives to serving other living beings," she said, "they cannot help but start asking questions about their own dedication and the meaning of it all." At the same time, she strongly reminded me that, at UWest, religious views are neither required, nor expected.

According to my observations, a definite educational benefit that results from regular interactions between dedicated monastics and secular students is that students, most of whom are very young, learn a great deal about monastics, who are usually elderly people. Because the latter exemplify patience, compassion, wisdom, and loving kindness, students develop respect for the elderly, and I strongly believe that this is an extremely important aspect of education, especially against the background of modern culture in the United States, where the elderly are sometimes pushed aside and even mocked (especially when they are driving).

Significantly, multicultural aspects of the UWest education also come from nuns and monks. They arrive from more than 30 different countries and participate in all university and temple activities. Their regular participation in the university's events provides for the well-structured and coherent reference to many different cultures with their distinct food, music, and political-cultural history. Some of the Buddhist traditions that have been oppressed, or destroyed during the last century, such as those of Tibet and Nepal, get a second chance at UWest. Through public support, these traditions become revitalized, and students get a chance to observe the process of cultural restoration. Moreover, they get a chance to directly participate in it, and they begin to feel that they are making history. This provides for an optimistic outlook on society and gives students hope that positive changes and reparations are still possible. When political and religious leaders from different countries come to the Hsi Lai Temple to discuss the future of humanity, students attend these meetings and learn how to take responsibility for the world, not just their own educations and careers.

STUDENTS AT THE UNIVERSITY OF THE WEST

UWest has an extremely diverse student body. Currently, there are 54 percent domestic and 46 percent international students, and these international students come from more than 30 different countries. One characteristic feature of student body at UWest is that it includes both monastic and secular students. This combination of two types of students, those who have taken full monastic vows, and those who remain secular, but practice meditation and certain forms of Buddhist ethical behavior, creates a unique learning atmosphere on campus. Monastics encourage other students to become vegetarian, avoid harming animals, and protect the natural environment. They help non-religious students with meditation practices and strengthen their moral behavior, especially in personal relationships with each other.

Students interviewed for this book explained why they had chosen UWest instead of other universities—the great majority (close to 90 percent) have chosen UWest because of the moral climate on its campus; they specified that what they liked about it is that there is no crime, no violence, and no unpleasant people (bullies) to be encountered. All students, without exception, reported that the most important impression they have from the university and its campus is that all people are "very kind and help each other." A good proportion of students (nearly 50 percent) reported they had chosen UWest in order to learn "how to be non-materialistic," "stop being greedy," and "to be fair to others." The reason given rather often for choosing UWest is that students wanted to learn how to help others, take care of the environment, and learn how to live like a community. Some students suggested that, if everyone in the world received education at the UWest, the crisis of 2008 would not have happened. The education they receive, they said, really makes a difference in a person's life and is exactly the kind of education the whole world needs right now.

In 2013, I interviewed Jacob Sky, a recent graduate of the UWest. I asked him, "What is the most important Buddhist value you have learned during your years as a student?" This is what he told me:

> The most important thing I have learned pertains to my new understanding of human consciousness. As I see it now, there are two types of knowledge. One is abstract and theoretical, and we may call it purely scientific. This is the knowledge in which the knower, the known, and the knowing are separated from each other. In other words, the investigator of the outside world looks at this world as merely an object of his study, entirely separate from his own life, his emotional commitments, and his character traits. This theoretical knowledge is not centered on the problem of human well-being and the well-being of the community. Another type of knowledge can be called the Buddhist-based consciousness. This is the inter-subjective approach in which the learner understands that he has an impact on that which he learns, and at the same time, that which he learns is impacting him. It is called "Direct Perception." When used as a main method in all forms of study, it produces a very powerful effect. A good way to understand this will be to point at a difference between simply talking about all possible qualities of an apple, without ever tasting it, versus eating different kinds of apples regularly while studying their qualities at the same time.
>
> Western culture equates knowledge with our ability to talk about things, to remember things, to report on things. But in the Buddhist-based methodology, while all of these aspects are present, there is one additional aspect lacking in Western education: daily personal practice of all things the student has learned. We call it "Constant Mindfulness," and "Active Engagement with Learning." My study at UWest taught me to constantly remember that, as I learn—I change, and as I change—I learn. And the more I learn and change, the more impact I have on my own life and the life of the entire human community. To me, this is the highest value of the Buddhist-based education.

NOTES

1. Some examples: Boston University built a twenty-six-story glass-and-steel tower for a student dormitory, and there are floor-length mirrors inside each room. Drexel University spent $45 million for an 84,000-square-foot recreation center. High Point University provides outdoor hot-tubs, water-falls, and pool-slides, and there is a concierge desk where students make restaurant reservations, send out dry cleaning, and drop off library books.

2. One particular way which makes taking care of the cafeteria inexpensive is students' behavior. After they are done eating, they clean food remains from the surface of the dishes by using the same napkin they used during the meal. They sort things out; that is, cups go into one stack, chopsticks go into a container with warm soapy water, etc. Students clean after them-

selves as it is done in the Buddhist monasteries. Food leftovers are very few as students have already learned not to take more than they will eat.

3. Academic benefits of "on-campus mingling" between secular students and monastics is explained later in this chapter.

4. His name is also transliterated as Hsing Yun.

5. Also transliterated as Foguang shan.

6. Manure was used as fuel in rural China, so little Xingyun sold it for a few coins to help his family.

7. This particular trait—accepting animals as fellow beings on the way to enlightenment—Xingyun shares with another Chinese master—Xuan Hua, founder of the Dharma Realm Buddhist University whose life is examined in the next chapter. Some people still remember how Xuan Hua had rescued forty pigeons in the San Francisco Buddhist Lecture Hall. These pigeons were released during the "Liberating Life Ceremony," but several of them refused to fly away. These remaining pigeons followed Xuan Hua wherever he went and carefully "listened" to his sermons.

8. "Diamond Sutra is one of the most important Mahayana texts. It was written in Sanskrit approximately between the 2nd and 4th centuries and translated to Chinese as early as the 5th century. This sutra is one of the "perfection of wisdom" text (prajna-paramita) and, according to Gregory Schopen, its contents were meant to "rearrange, or shutter established ways of seeing the world and conventional religious practices."

9. It is known today as the Nanjing Massacre of 1937.

10. After doing this for so many years, this has become his habit. Someone saved a later sample of such completely worn out, but repaired with the cardboard, shoes. I saw them at the exhibit in the Foguangshan History Museum in Taiwan.

11. Tripitaka is the name of the Buddhist canon. It is a Sanskrit word and literally means "Three Baskets." Buddhist canon received this name because it is divided into three parts, or baskets, each containing a particular type of the Buddha's instructions. The first part, or basket, contains stories about the Buddha himself and is called Sutra-pitaka; the second part contains the Buddha's instructions to nuns and monks on how to behave in order to avoid creating attachments and is called Vinaya-pitaka; and the third part that was created later than the other two contains commentaries and is called Abhidharma-pitaka. For a detailed history of the Chinese Tripitaka, see Storch.

12. It is a historical irony that these forty monks were ordered to receive military training after their arrival in Taiwan. Commander General Sun Li-jen (1899–1990) insisted that if monks wished to participate in the army-relief effort, they had to be properly trained!

13. To this day, he remembers the joy of that moment. When we recall how good a calligrapher he is and how much he appreciates the "Art of the Brush," we can understand his feelings. Hundreds of his calligraphy-pieces are exhibited around the world, including University of the West Museum and Museum of Buddhist Art in Foguangshan, Taiwan.

14. Because of his literary accomplishments, he was later invited to serve as Dean of Education at the Taiwan Buddhist Training Institute.

15. One of the imprisonments lasted 23 days during which he was not allowed to lie down and rest, but remained bound and restrained; he was treated with open brutality.

16. This museum is located in Foguangshan headquarters near the city of Kaohsiung in Taiwan.

17. According to traditional disciplinary rules, monks and nuns are not allowed to sing, only chant. Yet, knowing that singing is such a big part of Chinese culture, Xingyun decided to create a new form of devotion—composing and singing new popular songs which exemplified and propagated Buddhist ideals.

18. Stuart Chandler dedicates a chapter of *Establishing a Pure Land on Earth* to a discussion of the Foguang Humanistic Buddhism and its distinct characteristics (Chandler, 43–77).

19. He insisted that education must be free for all people.

20. "Triple gem," or "Triratna" in Sanskrit, is also translated as "Three Jewels." It refers to a Buddhist concept of "taking refuge in," that is, "receiving help from," three most precious gifts—Buddha, Dharma, and Sangha. "Buddha" refers to the historical Buddha, "Dharma"

refers to his teachings, and "Sangha" refers to a community of practitioners including both monastic and lay people.

21. Theravada, literally, "The Path of the Elderly," denotes the oldest form of Buddhism—the one that requires monastic experience for full liberation. Mahayana, literally, "Large Vehicle" embraces the later teachings in which salvation from suffering is promised to everyone who practices regardless of whether they remain in society or retreat into a monastery. Vajrayana, "Diamond Vehicle," is usually applied to Tibetan forms of Buddhism, which provide salvation in this lifetime if a practitioner specifically follows a path of tantric practices designed by the guru.

22. The campus is located in Rosemead. It takes about 15 minutes by car to travel from the university to the temple.

23. See Yung for a detailed examination of classical and modern Buddhist ideas on economic wealth.

24. For information on most recent scholarships, see Fisher.

REFERENCES FOR CHAPTER ONE

Chandler, Stuart. 2004. *Establishing a Pure Land on Earth; The Foguangshan Buddhist Perspective on Modernization and Globalization*. Honolulu: Hawaii University Press.

Fisher, Danny. 2010. "University of the West Celebrates $1.1 Million in Scholarships for Buddhist Studies," http://dannyfisher.org/2010/02/02

Fu, Zhiying. 2008. *Bright Star, Luminous Cloud: The Life of a Simple Monk*, translated by Robert Smitheram. Hacienda Heights, CA: Buddha Light Publishing.

Hsing Yun. 2006a. *Core Teachings: Buddhist Practice and Progress*. Hacienda Heights, CA: Buddha Light Publishing.

———. 2008. *Humanistic Buddhism*. Hacienda Heights, CA: Buddha Light Publishing.

———. 2006b. *A Look at Modern Issues: Buddhism and Our Changing Society*. Hacienda Heights, CA: Buddha Light Publishing.

Hsu, Tai. 2010. "Humanistic Buddhism." Hacienda Heights, CA: Foguang Shan Hsi Lai Temple.

I.B.P.S., Buddhist Memorial Complex. 2010. *The Ultimate Care*. Hacienda Heights, CA: Buddha Light Publishing.

Kosareff, Jason. 2011. "University of the West Participates in Rosemead Water Recycling Project," *Buddhist News*: http://www.uwest.edu/site

Lin, Irene. 2006. "Journey to the Far West: Chinese Buddhism in America," in Tanya Storch (ed.) *Religions and Missionaries in the Pacific, 1500–1900*. Aldershot, UK: Ashgate Publishing, Ltd.

Master Xingyun. 2012. *Bells, Gongs and Wooden Fish*. Hacienda Heights, CA: Buddha Light Publishing.

———. 1999. *Humble Table, Wise Fare: Hospitality for the Heart*, translated by Tom Manzo and Dr. Shujan Cheng. Rosemead: Hsi Lai University Press.

———. 2006. *The Light of Hope*, translated by Cathie Chen. Burlingame: Buddhist Text Translation Society.

McDonald, Raymond. 2013. "Second Overnight Sit Builds Diverse Sangha at UWest," *University of the West Student Government*: http://www.uwsa.net/current-business.

Miller, Andrea. 2008. "Profile: The University of the West," *Buddhadharma: The Practitioner's Quarterly*. http://thebuddhadharma.com/issuees/2008/fall/profile.

Newton, Edmund. 1988. "Buddhists Concentrate Hsi Lai Temple," *Los Angeles Times*.

Selingo, Jeffrey. 2013. *College (Un)bound: The Future of Higher Education and What it Means for Students*. Boston: New Harvest.

Storch, Tanya. 2014. *The History of Chinese Buddhist Bibliography: Censorship and Transformation of the Tripitaka*. New York: Cambria Press.

Xuan, Pan. 2013. *Buddha-Land in the Human World*. Hacienda Heights, CA: Buddha Light Publishing.

Yung, Dong. 2006. "Chinese Buddhism and Economic Progress," *Hsi Lai Journal of Humanistic Buddhism* 7: 264-278.

Chapter Two

The Dharma Realm
Buddhist University

FIRST ENCOUNTER

To reach Dharma Realm Buddhist University (DRBU), I took picturesque Highway One in California and drove north toward Ukiah. It is near Ukiah that I found the City of Ten Thousand Buddhas[1]—a place worth travelling to and exploring for a whole day regardless of whether one has a specific interest in the history of Dharma Realm Buddhist University.

The land for the City of Ten Thousand Buddhas was purchased in 1976 by the students of Master Xuan Hua[2] whose life I describe in a following segment of this chapter and who is regarded by everyone as the founder of the DRBU. The space is huge—448 acres consisting of meadows, groves, and foothills. In addition, there are twenty-five institutional buildings on the land, including "Instilling Goodness" Elementary School, "Developing Virtue" Secondary School, "Joyous Giving" housing for nuns, and the "Tahagata Monastery" housing for monks. Numerous orchards and vegetable fields are spread around—most of the food consumed in the City of Ten Thousand Buddhas, including food served at the university's dining hall, is grown here (CTTB 2011a).

As at UWest, a visitor to DRBU meets different types of Buddhist monastics who come from both Asian and European countries. But unlike on the UWest campus, at the Dharma Realm Buddhist University, secular students do not live in the same dormitories as the monastics, albeit the two groups freely mingle and interact in other areas. The DRBU's campus is a unique place and beautiful beyond words. The moment I walked through the golden gate separating the City of Ten Thousand Buddhas from the residential area of Ukiah, I was immediately affected by stereophonic sound of peacocks. With their fan-like tails fully opened, glittering brightly in the light, they walked slowly toward me, shrieking in their high-pitched voices a welcome to a new visitor. Next to the birds, looking humble in their grey and brown robes, Korean and Chinese nuns walked slowly, mindfully, in the same direction.

The presence of animal life, peacefully co-existing with humans, while the university's community provides full psychological and material support, is typical of all Buddhist-based universities. Respectful treatment of animals is consistent with the teachings of Buddhism because, according to its traditional classification of life-forms, animals are capable of reaching the enlightenment and are only one level below humans.[3] Much like us, they can realize their Buddha-nature, and it is this perspective on the animal's consciousness that is the main reason for vegetarianism observed on most Buddhist campuses including the DRBU. This constant presence of animals also serves as an invitation for the compassionate treatment of all living beings and reminds us of the interconnectedness of all life (Epstein 2014).

As I continued walking around the DRBU campus, I realized that teachings of enlightenment and compassion were present in the surroundings in a very physical way. I noticed wooden poles with arrows that guide visitors around the campus. One of the arrows read: "Avenue of Compassion;" another arrow invited me to the "Walk of Kindness;" yet another pointed to the "Patience Street." I soon found out that these were actual addresses on campus. As one can imagine, just by thinking that I was walking on the Avenue of Compassion, I began developing a degree of sympathy and kindness toward my surroundings and became more mindful of what to say and do. When I saw a smiling woodpecker atop of the arrow, which pointed to the "Joyous Way," I think I experienced a moment of enlightenment.

LIFE OF MASTER XUAN HUA,
FOUNDER OF THE DHARMA REALM BUDDHIST UNIVERSITY

The most complete and reliable source of information about Master Xuan Hua's life is a two-volume collection, *In Memory of the Venerable Master Hsuan Hua* published in 1995 by the Buddhist Text Translation Society (BTTS 1995). This impressive collection of materials is in two languages, English and Chinese. The first volume is comprised of three parts: "His Life," "His Contributions," and "His Teachings;" the second volume contains photographic materials including pictures of Master Hua, his personal objects and sacred artifacts used in religious ceremonies, pieces of poetry and calligraphy he composed during his life, and a collection of his speeches, prayers, and lectures.

The early years of Xuan Hua's life are not very well known. If we rely on the information recorded by his American followers, he was born around 1918 in a small village near Harbin in northeast China (Shuangchang County, Jilin Province). He was the youngest of ten children, and his mother, like the mother of Xingyun, founder of the UWest, was a devout Buddhist. She was a vegetarian and recited the name of the Buddha Amitabha her entire life.[4] When Xuan Hua was merely a little boy, he already followed his mother's example—he ate only vegetarian food and recited the Buddha's name. There is a recollected story of his experience of awakening at age eleven after seeing a dead baby, but not becoming a monk at this point because his mother had asked him to wait until her death (BTTS 1995, 9–10).[5]

Even though Xuan Hua could not become a monk at that time, he obtained his parents' permission to travel in search of his spiritual teacher. Because his family was poor, he could not afford to go to school until he turned fifteen. But when he finally entered the school, he learned everything so rapidly that, by age sixteen, he was already able to lecture on Buddhist sutras to village people. His students report that, in addition to Buddhist texts, Master Xuan Hua memorized the entire Confucian canon consisting of the Four Books and Five Classics.[6] He also became sufficiently versed in traditional Chinese medicine, astrology, divination, and physiognomy, and read scriptures of a native Chinese religion—Daoism. At seventeen, he established a free school where he taught thirty impoverished children and adults. When he turned eighteen, he found himself obligated to return home to care for his terminally ill mother.

His mother died when he was nineteen. For three years after her death, he observed a full mourning ritual, and it was during that time, as he sat by her grave in a state of deep mournful meditation, that he received a vision with profound implications. He saw Huineng (638–713), the Sixth Patriarch of the Chan School,[7] who walked toward him and told him he must go to the West and help the "white people" realize their Buddha-nature.

As a monk, he was given his first Dharma name: Anci, which means "Peace and Compassion." One of his first teachers, Master Chang Zhi, transmitted to him the Pilu lineage of the Chan School. During his training, Xuan Hua actively dedicated himself to the mastery of meditation and the study of Buddhist scriptures, which is typical of the Chinese Chan traditions. In 1946, he began a long journey south where he had hoped to receive full ordination on holy Mt. Putuoshan. In 1948, after travelling two thousand miles, he arrived at the Nanhua monastery where he trained extensively with the most revered and enlightened Chan-master of that time, Xuyun (1880–1959). From him he received the mind-seal transmission in the Weiyang lineage, and it was during that time that he received his second Dharma name: Xuan Hua, which means "To Proclaim and Transform" (BTTS 1995, 10–12).

Following his earlier vision, revealing that he must spread Buddhism in the West, Xuan Hua moved to Hong Kong in 1949. This saved him from persecution in the hands of the Chinese communists, although this was not his main goal in leaving China behind. In Hong Kong, he taught meditation and lectured on various Buddhist texts, simultaneously sponsoring these texts' modern printed editions. He assisted refugees from mainland China in any way he could. He helped Buddhism remain a vital tradition outside of China by keeping it relative to the lives of ordinary people. In this, he was once again, rather similar to Master Xingyun, the founder of UWest whose biography was detailed in the previous chapter.

While in Hong Kong, Xuan Hua was busy with a whole range of activities. He established the "Buddha Lecture Hall," renovated "Flourishing Compassion Monastery," and built the "Western Bliss Garden Monastery." He raised funds for and commissioned several Buddhist statues, insisting that the sculptors follow the artistic standards of the Tang (618–907), Song (960–1279), and Ming (1368–1644) dynasties which, to him, embodied classical forms of the Chinese Buddhist statuary. His intention was to ensure that visual arts in the Chinese Buddhist traditions remained true to their historical roots and keep religious-philosophical foundations intact.[8]

In 1962, Xuan Hua made the decision to immigrate to the United States. He responded to the urges of his former Hong Kong disciples, who had by now settled in the Bay Area of Northern California. Soon after his arrival, he opened the "Buddha Lecture Hall" in San Francisco, following the example of an institution he had headed in Hong Kong. Initially, it was established and functioned merely as a branch of the Buddhist Lecture Hall of Hong Kong, but a community of the American Buddhist practitioners associated with the Buddhist Lecture Hall grew so rapidly that the name had to be changed, first, to the "Sino-American Buddhist Association," and then to the "Dharma Realm Buddhist Association" (BTTS 2001, 7–25).

During his first years of teaching in San Francisco, Xuan Hua made contact with many Americans of European descent who wished to study Chan (Zen) form of Buddhism from the original Asian master. Some of these early disciples, such as Richard Baker, the first abbot of the San Francisco Zen Center, became rather famous and influential in the world of American contemporary Buddhism. Yet, according to Xuan Hua's other prominent disciple, Ronald Epstein, after initial success in teaching Americans of European descent, he needed to impose on himself a period of nearly complete social isolation. The isolation lasted from 1963 to 1968, and during this period, Xuan Hua's public teaching of the Dharma was virtually non-existent. The exact nature of the problem experienced by Xuan Hua with his non-Asian students is not fully known. Epstein characterizes it as resentment against the disrespectful behavior toward the Dharma. But in 1968, the isolation suddenly ended, and Xuan Hua began, once again, actively preaching and conducting public meditation sessions. A new feature was added to his activities during this time—full ordination ceremonies for the non-Asian American disciples. It can be suggested that by doing so Xuan Hua found a solution to the problem of "disrespectful behavior" often exhibited by this category of students. When they were offered a full monastic ordination (which was previously reserved for the Asian disciples), their behavior changed toward greater respect for the Sangha and its moral ideals.

In 1969, he astonished the monastic community of Taiwan by sending there two American women and three American men whom he had previously ordained as novices and who were expected to receive complete monastic ordination. These five people became the very first Americans to become fully ordained as Buddhist nuns and monks. During the subsequent years, Xuan Hua trained and ordained hundreds of people, both Asian and European Americans. In 1976, 1979, 1982, 1989, 1991, and 1992, he conducted full monastic ordinations across Oregon, Washington, and California. People came from all over the world to take part in these ceremonies. Those monastics who were ordained by him during these ceremonies are now teaching at the twenty-eight temples, monasteries, and convents in the United States, Canada, and East Asia (BTTS 2001, 13–14).

In respect to these ordinations, I must point to the noteworthy difference existing between this Chinese master and the Tibetan Lama Chogyam Trungpa, the founder of Naropa University, whose life will be examined in the next chapter. From Chogyam Trungpa's biography, it becomes clear that not every founder of a Buddhist-based university believed it was necessary to train students in some form of monastic discipline as a way of improving their consciousness and thus enriching their experience of education. But Xuan Hua definitely believed that such training was necessary and sought to establish a university that involved cooperation between the ordained monastics and secular students. His approach is aptly evident in the institutional structure of the Dharma Realm Buddhist University which, to this day, counts many more monks and nuns as members of administration, faculty, and student body than other Buddhist universities do.

Xuan Hua strongly believed that making good, reliable translations of Buddhist texts to modern languages, including modern English, must be a big part of Buddhist-inspired education. He is quoted as saying, "As soon as I became a monk, I looked into why so few people study Buddhism despite its undeniable principles . . . I discovered that it was because the disciples of the Buddha did not translate the Buddhist sutras into different [Western] languages" (BTTS 2001, 76).

Consequently, as early as 1968, he began a program for translation training and activities at the Buddhist Lecture Hall. By 1973, he had established the International Translation Institute on Washington Street in San Francisco, where it had successfully functioned until it merged with the Dharma Realm Buddhist University in 1977. Today, the Buddhist Text Translation Society is located in Burlingame, CA. Although it exists independently from the DRBU, a whole set of degrees granted by the university is directly related to the Translation Institute's activities; while the DRBU students often serve as interns and work for the Translation Society after graduation (BTTS 2001, 74–82).

Xuan Hua played an unprecedented role in spreading the Chinese Mahayana tradition in the United States and across Northern America. Here are just a few examples:

He established the Gold Mountain Dhyana Monastery in San Francisco, Gold Wheel Monastery in Los Angeles, Bodhidharma Center and Gold Summit Monastery in Seattle, Avatamsaka Monastery in Calgary, and Gold Buddha Mountain Monastery in Vancouver (BTTS 1995, 17).

He promoted Buddhist-inspired education at all levels and for all ages, which is evident from the inauguration of the "Instilling Goodness" elementary school in San Francisco (1976) and "Developing Virtue" secondary school in The City of Ten Thousand Buddhas (1980).

His international activities for the sake of propagating Buddhist teachings and strengthening moral education in Asia were equally important. In 1974, he led a delegation to Hong Kong, India, Singapore, Vietnam, and Taiwan, with the purpose of exchanging Buddhist ideas and restoring moral dimensions in Asian education. In 1978, he led a delegation to Malaysia where he supervised the "Triple Gem" ordination in which 6,000 people participated.[9]

Xuan Hua cared deeply about the suffering of Asian refugees and the looming ecological crisis in Asia. To help, in 1986, he established a Buddhist Council for the Rescue and Resettlement of Refugees and signed an agreement with the U.S. government allowing children of Asian refugees to receive free board and education in the City of Ten Thousand Buddhas. To raise awareness of the dangers posed by humans to the environment, he hosted "Water, Land, and Air," a ceremony to which he invited 100 officials from the People's Republic of China, using this as an opportunity to discuss ecological problems.

Like the Master Xingyun, founder of UWest, Xuan Hua believed in a multi-faith approach to the problems which modern humanity was facing; he actively sought to eradicate religious hatred and sectarianism. Quoting from "A Portrait of the Venerable Master Hsuan Hua," "[he] insisted on ecumenical respect, and he delighted in interfaith dialogue. He stressed commonalities in religious traditions—above all their emphasis on proper conduct, compassion, and wisdom. He was also a pioneer in building bridges between different Buddhist national traditions. He often brought monks from Theravada countries to California to share the duties of transmitting the precepts of ordination. He invited Catholic priests to celebrate the Mass in the Buddha Hall at the City of Ten Thousand Buddhas, and he developed a late-in-life friendship with Cardinal Paul Yu Bin, the exiled leader of the Catholic Church in China" (Epstein 2010). As a part of this mission which became his life-long commitment, he actively participated in the inter-religious dialogues with Christians, Jews, Muslims, and Hindus. Through the Conference of the United World Religions, he met authoritative teachers from the Christian, Islamic, Daoist, and Confucian communities and discussed with them such topics as universal ethics, safe development of sciences, and the prevention of technology's "taking-over" humanity. He was a regular speaker at the Buddhist-Christian conferences at the University of California in Berkeley.

More than anything, he worked tirelessly to bring moral education to his contemporaries because, for him, education in professional fields that was not accompanied by ethical development was dangerous. In his view, developing tremendous technological capabilities without developing a strong moral responsibility for its effects on people and nature is destined to create not a society of economic prosperity, but a global human catastrophe. Addressing this fundamental human problem, he lectured at the University of British

Columbia in Vancouver, the Quaker Center for Study and Meditation in Philadelphia, the University of Oregon in Portland, the University of Hawaii in Honolulu, the University of Minnesota in Minneapolis, the University of Georgia in Atlanta, and a dozen other universities, colleges, religious communities, and spiritual centers.

During his life, Xuan Hua followed monastic discipline; that is, he slept on a hard narrow bed and ate exclusively vegetarian food, and wore his monastic cloak no matter what the occasion. Nevertheless, he did not shy away from interactions with those who were far removed from his monastic environment, such as the influential political people of his time, especially if he saw an opportunity to do moral good. For instance, he agreed to be sworn as Chaplain of the San Francisco Police Department and accepted George H. W. Bush's invitation to attend the President's Dinner in Washington, D.C.[10] He accepted an invitation to attend the inaugural ceremonies of Governor Pete Wilson of California, and this was, in fact, the first time in American history that a Buddhist monk spoke at the inaugural ceremony for a state governor.

When Master Xuan Hua died in Los Angeles on June 7, 1995, his disciples and members of the Dharma Realm Buddhist Association held a 49-day session of the sutra-reciting in his honor. His body was cremated in the City of Ten Thousand Buddhas.

INSTITUTIONAL HISTORY AND ACADEMIC PROGRAMS OF THE DHARMA REALM BUDDHIST UNIVERSITY

The institutional goals of the Dharma Realm Buddhist University (DRBU) are drawn to make a statement that this university does not merely transmit academic knowledge, but creates a foundation for developing moral virtues, such as loving kindness, compassion, forgiveness, cooperation, and respect for all life. These goals further emphasize DRBU's commitment to promoting a spirit of shared inquiry and free exchange of ideas and that its faculty and students alike strive to exemplify scholarship and character in the seriousness of their study and solid life-practice. Intellectual inquiry at DRBU must proceed side by side with moral-spiritual cultivation, so that the classroom is inspired by contemplative life. Ultimately, this university promotes and supports the universal human capacity for inherent wisdom and moral goodness, while its flexible programs and contemplative atmosphere offer a chance to pursue personal growth and inner enrichment.[11]

The DRBU was founded in 1976, and its first programs were created during the late seventies and early eighties with the direct participation from its founder, Master Xuan Hua. The earliest degrees were in creative and practical arts, translation, Chinese language and culture, Buddhist studies, and religious studies. In the following period, the university continued offering a BA in translation and language studies, Buddhist study and practice, and Chinese studies, and a master's in translation and language studies, Buddhist study and practice, religious studies, and education.

During the last four to five years, the DRBU has undergone a significant transformation. During an interview in 2010, Dharma Master Venerable Heng Yi explained that the university is in a state of transition and that its faculty aim to create a wide-range, fully integrated, Buddhist-inspired education in liberal arts. The 2012–2013 general catalog continued to offer a bachelor's degree with concentration in one or two of the traditional DRBU areas, such as Buddhist study and practice, Buddhist education, Chinese studies, communication, English studies, Shastra studies,[12] Sanskrit studies, or Sutra studies;[13] but the most recent, 2015–2016, catalog features two fully integrated programs—a BA in liberal arts and an MA in Eastern and Western classics.

Based on my conversation with Wayne Chen, director of Development and Strategic Planning, discussions about changing the old format of education at the DRBU began in 2008–2009, when senior disciples of Master Xuan Hua came together and began asking questions about the value of Buddhist-based education in modern society. According to Wayne Chen, several underlying principles have been considered in the process: 1) The university aims to become a fully accredited institution under WASC; 2) The programs shall strive toward realizing the vision and aspiration set forth by the founder, Master Xuan Hua; 3) As a community dedicated to liberal education in the broad Buddhist tradition, DRBU is a place of study and practice for students of various religious backgrounds; 4) The central pedagogy aims to convey knowledge and activate intrinsic wisdom possessed by all individuals; and 5) The new text-based fully-integrated curriculum is a variation of the "Great Books" model championed by St. John's college and Thomas Aquinas College.

The results of many months of debates over these and other related issues are now fully expressed in the new curriculum. The following quote from the 2015–2016 catalog explains:

> The University offers an integrated curriculum that weaves together nine distinct strands: Buddhist Classics, Western Classics, Indian Classics, Chinese classics, Language, Mathematics, Natural Science, Rhetoric and Writing, and Music. The core curriculum consists of primary texts—Buddhist, Western, Indian, and Chinese Classics—studied and discussed in a pro-seminar setting, conducted in the spirit of shared interpretive inquiry. Through a close reading of primary classics, students are able to enter into the dynamic dialogues from which many of these texts emerged. They engage the material more intimately, as if sitting as participant-observers in discourses that stimulated critical inquiry and self-reflection then and reanimate it now. The lively and trenchant

quality of the classic text connects students not only to the "voice" and energy of the author, but often also invigorates them to re-examine their own capacities, goals, questions, and concerns. The direct encounter with an original source can often trigger a re-examination of assumptions and presuppositions—personal and cultural—about human nature and our place in the world. A focus on classical texts thus provides a foundation for lifelong pursuit of learning, ever-deepening inquiry, and self-reflection.

Let us now briefly examine the selections of classics and the learning outcomes expected from studying them. The Western Classics sample reading list includes works by Homer, Sophocles, Plato, Aristotle, Virgil, Dante, Shakespeare, Descartes, Hume, Spenser, Austen, Emerson, Thoreau, Eliot, Heidegger, Hegel, Dostoevsky, Goethe, and Tocqueville. The expected outcomes are to better equip students to understand their own reactions to life circumstances at play and interplay between the personal, social, and natural worlds. The major focus of the Western classics strand is to take a student through a personal encounter with seminal Western thinkers, follow the development of knowledge in Western societies over a period of time, and identify with its dialectical nature and pursuit of truth.

A list of Buddhist classics is represented by philosophical treatises of Nagarjuna[14] and Vasubandhu,[15] two prominent philosophers of the early mature phase of Buddhism (second–fifth centuries); an impressive array of the Mahayana, or "Great Vehicle," tradition's most influential sutras such as the Nirvana-sutra, Lotus-sutra, Heart-sutra, Vimalakirti-sutra, Avatamsaka-sutra, and Sukhavativyuha-sutra; and the entirety of the Nikaya collections of texts which are Pali language-based.[16] Through the study of this set of classics, students are expected to master a dynamic fusion of theory and praxis because the very nature of the Buddhist classics is to simultaneously inform the mind and to build a moral character, that is to say, both explaining and engaging so as to ultimately lead human beings toward a fuller development of consciousness, moral will, and practical compassion.

The Indian classics list suggests readings from the Vedas, Brahmanas, and Upanishads, also including the Shankara's *A Thousand Teachings*, selected pieces from *The Complete Works of Swami Vivekananda*, Patanjali's *Yoga Sutras*, Valmiki's *Ramayana*, Gandhi's *The Story of My Experiments with Truth*, and several other seminal texts of Indian philosophy and literature that are less known to Western readers. Through the close reading of these texts, students are expected to learn about issues fundamental to the Indian understanding of past karmic influences on experiences of the present and future, reflect on the intricate relationship between language and reality, and gain an insight into causation as a force present at all levels of human activity. The Indian classics enable students to explore distinct South Asian perspectives on truth, freedom, and paths of salvation, as well as to develop a sincere appreciation for these texts, while critically evaluating them.

By looking at the Chinese classics sample list, I find that it features works by Confucius, Mencius, Xunzi, Zhuangzi, and a few other philosophers representing different influential schools of moral-political thought during the seminal period of Chinese civilization known as the Zhou dynasty (1122–256 BCE). It also includes texts which the Chinese people themselves have been referring to for centuries as classics, such as *Classic of Changes* (Yijing) and *Classic of History* (Shujing). It also includes great examples of poetry, such as Tang dynasty works, and famous novels of the medieval period, such as *Romance of the Three Kingdoms*. The Chinese classics strand expects students to ponder such questions as: What is an ideal of a good moral person? What does it mean to have a good government? What are the virtues? How should we relate to other people while pursuing personal cultivation? Students become familiar with a range of Chinese answers to these pressing questions and familiarize themselves with the Daoist and Confucian methods of self-cultivation. According to the "Curriculum," "Chinese classics strand is crucial to DRBU's mission to equip students with the necessary skills for understanding life in the globalized and multi-cultural world; it provides them with an increased range of resources with which to address pressing issues of modern society while allowing the appreciation of a diversity of worldviews."

This new emphasis on a global approach to culture, literature, and language through the study of classics from four different areas (Chinese, Western, Indian, and Buddhist) is the DRBU's new and original way of teaching Liberal Arts. The Dean of Academics, Dr. Martin Verhoeven, explained that the meaning of Liberal Arts at the DRBU is not the same as at the more traditional colleges, but one of inner liberation and unlocking each student's potential for inherent wisdom, free will, and a lifelong capacity to study on one's own, preparing for the new challenges of the ever-evolving world. According to him, students are invited to approach the great classics of the entirety of human civilization for the purpose of trying to understand their authors' minds, engage in inter-cultural dialogue, and develop a passion for deep, congenial, life-long learning. This process will, undoubtedly, shape the students' own intellects, and bring about their own emotional-intelligence-based responses of mutual understanding and compassion for other people— their lives, suffering, and search for meaning.

This unique process for learning the liberal arts is enhanced by having students enter and graduate from their programs all at the same time; and as they advance, they remain a part of the same, relatively small (ten to fifteen students) cohort. The grading process is, likewise, based on mutual understanding, cooperation, and congeniality. At the end of the semester, students come to a conference with several professors with whom they have studied and together they engage in a discussion of what each student has learned. This includes questions regarding how students can practically apply their

knowledge toward bettering themselves as morally responsible human beings, and how they will use their knowledge toward improving human relationships and local and global communities. Mere ability to "parrot" back the
contents of the classics learned in class is not considered knowledge. As
Ronald Epstein explained, "constant practice and deep personal understanding of everything one has learned" is the hallmark of the DRBU's way of
teaching and learning. "True knowledge is not abstract or theoretical," he
said, adding to this that, following master Xuan Hua's example, all teachers
and professors at the DRBU embody a morally responsible way of teaching
and learning—something so rarely seen in modern institutions of higher
learning.

Along with these impressive new beginnings, there still remain pieces of
the older programs which need to be transformed and integrated. For instance, in the past, of all Buddhist universities studied for this book, DRBU
offered the largest number of courses directly related to Buddhist practice,
such as Mantra Practice, Great Compassion Repentance, Guanyin Session,
Ten Thousand Buddhas Repentance, Door to Understanding the Hundred
Dharmas, Avatamsaka Sutra Recitation, Universal Bowing, Monastic Arts,
Daily Ceremonies, Selected Shastras, Daily Chan Meditation, Laity Precepts,
and Bodhisattva Precepts. Most of them were required for "Buddhist Study
and Practice" and "Buddhist Education" programs, but now these seem to be
gone (or suspended), replaced by Liberal Arts and Great Classics education.

While it remains to be seen how effective the new programs will be in
terms of making an impact on students' lives and their abilities to contribute
to the moral bettering of our society, it is easy to draw such conclusions for
the pre-existing programs. In particular, Buddhist Study and Practice has
been a unique program historically taught in Berkeley and the City of Ten
Thousand Buddhas. Based on conversations with the Venerables who designed it, the methods employed in this program involved mindfulness, compassion, and integration of study and practice. One of the nuns interviewed in
2010 said:

> Mindfulness is acquired through consistent meditation learned in such courses
> as Meditation for Beginners, Mantra Practice, and Avatamsaka Sutra Recita-
> tion. Students enrolled in Buddhist Study and Practice are required to partici-
> pate in an annual three-week retreat to advance their skills in mindful living,
> meditation, bowing, and chanting. These students often participate in tending
> to the garden and other types of meditation-like activities aimed at keeping the
> campus clean and beautiful. Such activities are similar to the nuns' and monks'
> daily practices in a typical Buddhist monastery.

Integration of study and practice has been traditionally pursued through
attending temple services and providing help on campus to those who need it.
In terms the academic subjects, students in the Buddhist Study and Prac-

tice program explained to me that they have been instructed to apply daily all aspects of knowledge learned in the classroom. For instance, one student made good use of a freshly learned Shakespeare sonnet (from an English Literature class) as a way of resolving some interpersonal conflict with his roommate. Another student helped elementary schoolchildren stop fighting with each other during the recesses by introducing them to meditation. In general, having asked people in Ukiah about the impact the DRBU has on their community, I learned that students were having a seriously positive effect through personal engagement, generously sharing knowledge received through classwork, and keeping the nearby area environmentally clean.

The main goal behind receiving a degree in Buddhist Study and Practice was to prepare for the challenges of the modern world and learn how to keep psychological balance while engaging in various social and professional activities. This particular program is closely associated with the vision of Xuan Hua who insisted that, in order to change our world for the better, we have to bring a complete change in people's consciousness and guide them toward developing personal virtue and serving communities of people rather than selfish interests. One of the instructors explained that students who take classes in Buddhist Study and Practice learn how to live their lives with presence, purpose and wisdom. She explained that students learn about a bodhisattva ideal of livelihood which motivates them to "bring everybody up" instead of pursuing narrowly defined "personal success." She concluded by saying: "The only correct motivation for giving and receiving knowledge is the wellbeing of all living beings." She also quoted Xuan Hua by saying, "There is no place that is not a classroom and nothing that is not a learning resource" (BTTS 1995, 27).

"Buddhist Education" was another separately distinguished program at DRBU which has now been partially converted into a strand within the new integrated liberal arts curriculum. Training specifically in the Buddhist forms of education has been proven, over the years, to be extremely useful for teachers in elementary, secondary, and high schools. Students pursuing this program also have the benefit of experiential learning rarely available at other universities—a chance to cooperate with and intern at the "Instilling Goodness" elementary and "Developing Virtue" secondary schools, both founded by Xuan Hua and located in the City of Ten Thousand Buddhas, practically joining the DRBU campus.

These two unusual schools deserve our attention for a moment because of their connection to Xuan Hua's vision for Buddhist-inspired education in the United States (DRBU 2001, 82–92; DRBU 2010–2012, 11–12).

The Instilling Goodness school opened in 1976 (the same year as the university) with the support of Carol Ruth Silver, San Francisco School Supervisor, and its first location was the International Translation Institute in San Francisco. In 1977–1978, the school moved to the City of Ten Thousand

Buddhas, the same location as the DRBU campus. Throughout its history, it has offered a fully bilingual program in Mandarin Chinese and English, while its educational practices (much like at the university) have been marked by a special emphasis on the importance of respecting parents and the elderly in the society. Instilling Goodness students are taught how to repay "social kindness" owed by the younger generations to the older generations.[17] At the same time, they are engaged in a state-approved curriculum in language, math, science, history, and physical education. Because this is a Buddhist-based school, they are also taught meditation, Tai Chi, traditional Chinese painting, and calligraphy (the same subjects, but at a higher level, have been traditionally offered at DRBU).

Developing Virtue secondary school opened in 1980. Like the elementary school and university, it combines in its curriculum requirements for academic excellence with special programs aimed at the cultivation of moral integrity in students. Educating how to respect parents and the elderly continues to be a big part of such programs; in addition, advanced classes are offered to teach young people how to become good citizens. They receive personalized guidance and are actively assisted by teachers and staff in seeking further education, preparing for careers in those fields which benefit the whole society and improve international relationships. "Boarding students do community service on weekends, such as cleaning the dining hall or participating in other organized community work. Through these chores, these future leaders of the country learn the habit of hard work . . . and increase their blessings through actual physical labor. . . . Parents of children, who exhibited the signs of being spoiled and self-indulgency, are pleasantly surprised to discover that their offspring have become more considerate and capable after staying in the City of Ten Thousand Buddhas" (BTTS 2001, 90–91).

Developing Virtue promotes separate education for girls and boys, which is somewhat similar to the gender-separated monastic dormitories in the City of Ten Thousand Buddhas. According to the school's charter, the separation was done to preserve the young students' innocence and make it easier for them to concentrate on their academic and moral study. Students are encouraged to "use the precious time of their youth to study well and develop their character instead of injuring themselves through the difficulties rising from premature emotional ties between the sexes" (BTTS 1995, 27).

The Dharma Realm Buddhist University and the two Buddhist-based schools for younger children have been historically connected. They share resources, space, founding principles, and most importantly, their founder's vision that education in America must be built on the formation of good moral character along with the mastery of technical skills and obtaining current scientific knowledge. Such character-building must be done in stages appropriate for a student's life, and if this is forgone for the sake of some other motives, the country will find itself in danger of moral corruption, and all the ideals of democracy will fail.

Many graduates from Instilling Goodness and Developing Virtues have historically enrolled in the DRBU, yet some have gone to Stanford, Berkeley, and MIT. Based on the interviews, regardless of their profession, they remain seriously committed to the principles they have learned through their earlier education, namely, respect for the elderly, humanness, and good citizenship. According to them, meditation and Buddhist studies train students to concentrate better and think more deeply and clearly. Additionally, because all meals are vegetarian they learn about the value of life, including the lives of animals. Students in both schools and at the university are held personally responsible for practicing moral principles, such as non-violence toward the environment and peace-making in personal conflicts. At a time when only a few states are capable of passing legislation curtailing sugary drinks at schools, the Buddhist-based schools teach and practice abstinence from corrupting one's consciousness by the use of alcohol, drugs and addictive substances such as sodas, cookies, and sugar-filled candies.

A degree in Buddhist Education has been proven to be useful for educators at all levels, especially for teachers in elementary and secondary schools. But it also provides a much wider range of training of equal importance to business managers, entrepreneurs, and community and social workers. The program set up and accomplished goals in human development that are in high demand in almost every area of our modern life. These goals are to: integrate theory and practice as essential components of higher learning; provide an integration of the ethical teachings of the Eastern and Western traditions; create dialogues between world religions and philosophies; and develop skills in evaluating and resolving conflict situations with wisdom and compassion.

Buddhist Education at DRBU, classified as psychological training, required nine units in comparative ethics and nine units in psychology for completing this program. Serious attention has been paid to the practical aspects of learning, and lessons in psychology and ethics were expected to be applied through "Practicum," which required twenty-four units and included training in daily and special-occasions ceremonies, as well as the mastery of Chan meditation, repentance practices, and sutra recitations (DRBU 2014).

Another outstanding program for which DRBU has been world famous, and which now has become a part of the integrated Liberal Arts, is "Translation and Language Studies" (BTTS 2001, 75–81). In the past, this program involved all aspects of translation from Chinese to English and from English to Chinese, with a special emphasis on scriptures and texts with moral and spiritual content. A similar program existed with respect to Japanese-English and English-Japanese translation. Although the DRBU no longer offers an MA in Translation and Language Studies, many talents and skills accumulated over many years of teaching it have been now applied toward language, rhetoric, writing, and various classics strands in the new BA and MA courses.

NOTES

1. The place is so called after the main Buddhist temple located here. This "Temple of Ten Thousand Buddhas" is, literally, decorated by ten thousand small Buddha-statues, each located in its own niche; the entirety of such niches covering space from floor to ceiling inside the temple. The design reminds us of famous grottos in northern China which, similarly, contain thousands of Buddha's images. The idea of multiplication and mutual reflection of the Buddha-nature in all phenomena is related to the Avatamsaka-sutra philosophy.

2. "This master's name has been interchangeably transliterated as Hsuan Hua and as Xuan Hua. Throughout this chapter, as well as throughout the book, I follow "pinyin" transliteration with a few exceptions in those cases in which pinyin was never applied. I apologize to those followers of Master Xuan Hua who prefer the other style of transliteration and are used to seeing their teacher's name spelled as Hsuan Hua. Yet, it is my academic conviction that the style of transliteration must be consistent throughout the monograph."

3. Life forms capable of the enlightenment include six main categories: deities, demons, humans, animals, hungry ghosts, and creatures of hells.

4. Amitabha, in Sanskrit, "Limitless Light," is the Buddha of the Western Pure Land and one of the most widely worshipped Buddhas in the Mahayana tradition. Followers of the Amitabha (Amida butsu, in Japanese), constitute a separate tradition often referred to as Amidism. For more on this, see James Foard et al., *The Pure Land Tradition*.

5. Although there is a genuine respect for and concern about one's own mother that is expressed in the life-stories of Xingyun and Xuan Hua, we must also remember that, in China, children needed their parents' permission in order to become a monk and join a monastery. When the permission was given by the parents, it still had to be approved by state authorities. See Storch.

6. Four Books include Confucius' *Analects*, *Mencius*, *Great Learning*, and *Doctrine of the Mean*. Five Classics include *Classic of Changes*, *Classic of Poetry*, *Classic of History*, *Records on the Rituals*, and *The Springs and Autumns Annals*.

7. A legendary image of Huineng is based on *The Platform Sutra of the Sixth Patriarch* (Liuzu tan jing) which dates from the late eighth century. In this text, Huineng is depicted as an illiterate poor man possessing unusual spiritual power. After he undergoes monastic training, he writes a verse in response to one written by Shenxiu (ca. 606–706), the central figure in the northern school of Chan. Because of this verse, Huineng received a secret ordination as the sixth patriarch of Chan. Chan lineages since the eight century identified with Huineng's ordination and accepted passing of the wisdom directly from him. For details, see McRae, John. 2003. *Seeing through Zen: Encounter, Transformation, and Genealogy in Chinese Chan Buddhism.* Berkeley: University of California Press.

8. Xingyun did similar things. He started dozens of museums of Buddhist art in Europe and Asia.

9. See the explanation of the Triple Gem ordination in footnote 19, in the biography of Xingyun.

10. "On April 28 he accepted the invitation of George Bush . . . and went with eighteen members of the Dharma Realm Buddhist Association to attend the President's Dinner . . . " (BTTS 1995, 21).

11. This is according to the DRBU official website.

12. Shastra is a Sanskrit term literally meaning "treatise." Shastra-literature embraces various forms of commentary written by Indian, Chinese, and Tibetan masters.

13. Sutras create a specific genre of Buddhist literature which describes events that happened in the Buddha's life, including his past lives. See footnote 14 in p. 22 where I explain the structure of the Buddhist canon.

14. Nagarjuna (ca. second century CE) explained philosophically the concept of Emptiness (shunyata). According to him, emptiness is a property possessed by each phenomenon due to that each phenomenon is a result of causal process and lacking the intrinsic existence of its own. He is the founder of the Madhyamaka, the earliest Mahayana form of Buddhism (Lindtner).

15. Vasubandhu (ca. mid-fourth to mid-fifth cc.) is primarily famous for his seven-hundred-stanza verse text entitled *Treasury of Abhidharma* (Abhidharmakosha). In this text, he presented the entirety of the contemporary doctrinal commentary tradition, or Abhidharma, by using logical format; he also used variant and sectarian interpretations of current terminology, offering lengthy arguments pro or con specific points. This text became essential in the Buddhist scholastic tradition of East Asia and Tibet and was used as textbook within monastic curricula. He is considered to be the founder (along with his brother Asanga) of the Yogachara school of logic within the Mahayana Buddhism (Anacker).

16. Nikaya is also referred to as Agama; it represents the oldest sections of the Sutra-pitaka—collection of Buddha's discourses. Usually, there are five such collections recognized: Collection of Long Discourses (Dighanikaya), Collection of Discourses of Middle Length (Majjhimanikaya), Connected Discourses (Samyuttanikaya), Discourses Increasing by One (Anguttaranikaya), and Collection of Small Discourses (Khuddhakanikaya). These collections are available and can be studied in several languages: Pali, Sanskrit, Tibetan, and Chinese (Hinüber).

17. This is a principle known as "Filial Piety," or "Xiao," in Chinese. Practically, all forms of Chinese Buddhism developed under serious influence from Confucian moral practices and doctrines.

REFERENCES FOR CHAPTER TWO

Anacker, Stefan. 1984. *Seven Works of Vasubandhu: The Buddhist Psychological Doctor.* Delhi: Motilal Banarsidas.
BTTS (Buddhist Text Translation Society). 1995. *In Memory of the Venerable Master Hsuan Hua.* Burlingame, CA: Buddhist Text Translation Society Press.
———. 2001. *Out of the Earth It Emerges: Wonderful Enlightenment Mountain.* Burlingame, CA: Buddhist Text Translation Society Press.
CTTB (City of Ten Thousand Buddhas). 2011a. "The Traditions of the City of Ten Thousand Buddhas," http://www.advite.com
———. 2011b. "Vegetarianism," http://www.advite.com
DRBU. 2001. *General Catalog 2001.*
———. 2010–2012. *General Catalog 2010–2012.*
———. 2014. *Spring 2014 Semester Course Schedule: Ukiah and Berkeley Campuses.*
Epstein, Ronald. 2006. "Buddhist Resources on Vegetarianism and Animal Welfare," www.sfsu.edu
———. 2010. "A Portrait of the Venerable Master Hsuan Hua," *Religion East and West* 10: 148–49.
———. 2014. "Resources for the Study of Buddhism," www.sfsu.edu
Flagg, Chuck. 2005. "The City of Ten Thousand Buddhas," *Morgan Hill Times.* March 20, 2011.
Foard, James, et al. (ed.). 1996. *The Pure Land Tradition: History and Development.* Berkeley: Regents of the University of California.
Hinüber, Oskar von. 1996. *A Handbook of Pali Literature.* Berlin and New York: de Gruyter.
Lindtner, Christian. 1982. *Nagarjuniana: Studies in the Writings and Philosophy of Nagarjuna.* Copenhagen, Denmark: Akademisk Forlag.
McRae, John. 2003. *Seeing through Zen: Encounter, Transformation, and Genealogy in Chinese Chan Buddhism.* Berkeley, CA: University of California Press.
Powers, Douglas. "Buddhism and Postmodernism," http://www.drbu.org/content
Storch, Tanya. 2000. "The Past Explains the Present: State Control Over Religious Communities in Medieval China." *The Medieval History Journal* 3, October.

Chapter Three

Naropa University

FIRST ENCOUNTER

Naropa University (NU) is located in Boulder, CO. My ride to the city of Boulder from the Denver airport was picturesque and memorable not only because of the Rocky Mountains dominating the landscape, but also because of the advanced technology on the freeways from Denver to my destination. Boulder impressed me even more by its well-developed environmental protection policies.

Unlike universities discussed in the previous chapters, Naropa University is spread across three campuses. For my "first encounter," I have chosen the campus on Arapahoe Avenue. It is relatively small, only 3.7 acres, but its grounds are esthetically beautiful and pleasant because of the mindful care given to them by the students. My attention was immediately drawn to the wide-open grassy space with a hill ring behind the Main Hall. When I inquired about its purpose, I was told that students, faculty, and administration use this space for the outdoor practices of meditation, yoga, Taich'i, and Kendo.

Waking around, I discovered that the campus provides many quiet places and tiny nooks for practicing meditation. Even a simple wooden table placed by the side of a building has been used for meditative practices. Every morning during my visit, I found rock formations made on the surface of that table. It was obvious—rocks were purposely balanced one on top of the other; sometimes, four or even five rocks have been balanced in this way, and the rocks' color-patterns seemed to have been deliberately chosen and juxtaposed. I detected the power of awareness and intention. I understood—it does not require large spaces to create the sense of beauty, awe, and respect for nature.[1]

I found another place for meditation and students' self-expression in the large nature-altar built on the side of the open grassy space. Plants, rocks, branches, flowers, and Buddhist images have been freely intertwined and are changed daily, even hourly. I realized, like the rocks on the table, the altar was touched by many hands, its objects moved around as an expression of sacred communion between nature and people on campus.

In another place, I found a tiny bench with one big rock by its side. The time of my visit coincided with the devastating oil-spill in the Gulf of Mexico. Across the solitary rock that stood by the bench, some student had written: AND THE OCEAN SIGHS—SPILL!!! What a powerful way, I thought, to express frustration and psychological pain without becoming violent.

I also saw traditional flags of Tibetan Buddhism proudly displayed around campus and many, many bicycles—one for each student enrolled in the university. I was told that every new student receives a free bicycle and annual pass for the city buses. Carbon-footprints on campus are being drastically minimized in this way, while students feel strongly—they are doing something important to protect mother-nature!

Despite the campus's small size, a list of the wonderful things created here is difficult to exhaust. To everything already mentioned, I must add a few words about the green-house. It is 22-foot-wide silver geodesic dome that looks as if it has just landed from space. The students proposed the building and it opened on Earth Day in 2009. Inside, permaculture, ikebana-art, and environment studies majors conduct their work. They also grow herbs and vegetables which are picked only minutes before they are added to soups and salads in the student cafeteria (Johnson).

LIFE OF TRUNGPA RINPOCHE, FOUNDER OF NAROPA UNIVERSITY

Chogyam Trungpa (1939–1987), who is often respectfully called Trungpa Rinpoche, described many events of his early life in his autobiography, *Born in Tibet* (Trungpa 2000a). In 2004, a close disciple, Fabrice Midal, published an account of his life titled *Chogyam Trungpa: His Life and Vision* which is generally accepted as most trustworthy by those who knew Chogyam Trungpa well (Midal). It is these two sources that I am using to outline Trungpa Rinpoche's biography.

He was born in February, 1939, in a small village on the high plateau of northeastern Tibet. His parents were nomads who raised yaks and sheep and constantly travelled from place to place. From Trungpa Rinpoche's own recollections, he did not see a single tree or bush until he left his village. He wrote, ". . . for the greater part of the year the whole land is under snow and it is so cold that the ice must be broken to get water" (Trungpa 2000a, 23).

He also recollected that on the night of his conception, his mother had a significant dream of a higher being entering her body with a flash of light;[2] and that in February, the month of his birth, flowers bloomed everywhere in the neighborhood, although it was still winter and the earth was covered with snow (Trungpa 2000a, 25).

At only thirteen months old, he was recognized as a tulku. Tulku, a term of Tibetan Buddhism, refers to the rebirth of an important master. The process by which Chogyam Trungpa was identified as a reborn master (or tulku) is described in great detail in Chapter One of *Born in Tibet*, "Found and Enthroned." The process was similar to that by which the fourteenth Dalai Lama was identified. Concretely, when the tenth guru—the last in the lineage of Trungpa Rinpoche—died, a hierarchical superior received a message in a dream that the rebirth of the departed master had already taken place in a village located a five-day walking distance from Surmang. The dream revealed other details: a house with a south-facing door, the family's large red dog, and the mother's and father's names. Chogyam Trungpa, as a small child, was found there in accordance with these signs and put to a test. From several similar objects, such as several walking sticks, bowls, and monk-robes, he had to select only those few things that belonged to his predecessor, the tenth guru of the Trungpa lineage. Chogyam successfully completed this task (Midal).

There are four major schools in Tibetan Buddhism: Nyingma, Sakya, Kagyu, and Geluk.[3] Of these, Chogyam Trungpa inherited two traditions—Kagyu and Nyingma, considered to be the oldest and having the most empha-sis on the Tantric teachings. In his reincarnation as the eleventh Trungpa, he was expected to be a religious-political leader of a group of monasteries in the Surmang district, and he was installed in a leadership position while he was still a child. Twelve thousand people, monks and lay Buddhists, attended the ceremony. According to eyewitnesses, when Chogyam's hair was about to be cut off during the ceremony, a blast of thunder roared and it began to rain; then, a rainbow appeared—all of this was considered to be very auspi-cious according to the traditional divination system of Tibet (Midal, 41–42).

Although he was already installed as the eleventh Trungpa, Chogyam continued living with his mother until he turned five. At this point, his training began in earnest. It took many years of studying with several distin-guished teachers and involved extremely hard personal work to shape the young boy's heart and mind according to all necessary requirements. He wrote later, "My own time-table was as follows: I rose up with my tutor at five for the first morning devotions, then we were given breakfast, after which my reading lessons went on till midday; this was followed by a meal and half and hour's rest. Then I was given a writing lesson for half an hour, and again reading until the evening" (Trungpa 2000a, 46). He also noted, "I had been brought up strictly from infancy . . . , so that I had no other reference point such as the idea of freedom or being loose. I had no idea what it was like to be an ordinary child playing in the dirt. . . . Since I did not have any other reference point I thought that was just the way the world was" (Trungpa 2000b, 97–98).

After the arduous training had been completed, it was time to assume full responsibility as a leader of the Surmang monasteries. Chogyam took it seriously and even decided to build a new seminary for his district. He explained: "Even if the Communists destroy the whole place, the seeds of knowledge in our hearts cannot be destroyed" (Trungpa 2000a, 100). Midal noted that "it is revealing that one of the first important decisions he made was to go against the inertia of the times and to try to renew the way the teachings were presented" (Midal, 54). However, in 1949, the Communist Party took control of China and a year later, in 1950, it publicly declared its determination to "liberate" Tibet from the "foreign imperialists." In 1955, persecution of Tibetan Buddhist clergy began in earnest, with hundreds of nuns and monks tortured and killed.

The fourteenth Dalai Lama fled to India four years after the persecution began, leaving Chogyam caught between two options. One option was to leave Tibet, like the Dalai Lama, and thus preserve the lineage he had received from his teachers. The other was to fulfill his religious-political duty requiring him to stay in Tibet and protect the monasteries entrusted to him through the sacred enthronement. After news reached him that Chinese troops had already opened and desecrated the tomb and body of the tenth Trungpa, and all treasures, altars, and scriptures in the main monastery had been destroyed, the decision was made. He had to go. His escape journey was long and dangerous; it lasted nearly ten months until he arrived in India in 1959.

He stayed in India from 1959 to 1963. While there, he was appointed by the Dalai Lama to serve as the spiritual advisor to the Young Lamas Home School, and he also had the chance to personally meet with Prime Minister Nehru and the President of India, Radhakrishnan. According to Chogyam's own words, "By contrast to the medieval world of Tibet, India was a very modern place. Here, for the first time, I had a contact with Westerners, and I realized it was absolutely necessary for me to study their language to spread the Dharma" (Trungpa 2000a, 251). Precisely because of this reasoning, he applied himself to studying English and was so successful in his endeavor that, with the help of Western scholars, he became a recipient of the Spalding sponsorship. In 1963, he went to study Comparative Religion at St. Anthony's College in Oxford, UK.

Trungpa Rinpoche's life in the West is well documented through his own speeches and writings recently published in *The Collected Works of Chogyam Trungpa*.[4] Additionally, several books were written in English by Western authors interested in preserving the legacy of his teaching in the UK and United States. Such works include but are not limited to Jeremy Hayward's *Warrior-King of Shambala*, Diana Mukpo's *Dragon Thunder: My Life with Chogyam Trungpa*, Jeffrey Paine's *Re-Enchantment: Tibetan Buddhism Comes to the West*, James Coleman's *The New Buddhism*, and Ram Dass's *It is Here Now*. According to these sources, his adaptation to English culture was very quick, and in just four years after arriving in the UK (in 1967), he had already established (together with Akong Rinpoche) the Samye Ling Monastery—the first Tibetan monastery in the Western hemisphere. Two years after that, in 1969, he became the first British Tibetan citizen.

In the middle of these positive developments, he was severely injured in a car accident which left him half-paralyzed. According to Trungpa's own admission, it was after that accident that he made a firm decision to renounce the monastic vows he had taken in Tibet.[5] His general approach to monastic traditions can be summarized through words he wrote a few years after he had officially renounced his monkhood: "Tradition does not mean dressing up in robes and playing exotic music or having dakinis dancing around us, or anything like that. Tradition is being faithful to what we have been taught and to our own integrity. From this point of view, tradition is being awake and open, welcoming but at the same time stubborn" (Midal, 84). His biographer offered a commentary to this, saying: "Thus, an authentic relationship with Tradition is a matter of purity of heart and not of being a conservative. It is inseparable from freedom to return, beyond all conventions, to the source" (Midal, 85).

After release from his monastic vows, Trungpa Rinpoche did not merely stop wearing a Tibetan robe, replacing it with Western clothes, but he began drinking whiskey, smoking cigarettes, and having sexual relationships with women; at the same time, he ignored many Western conventions of socially polite behavior. He has been viewed as controversial, but at the same time, his expressions of internal psychological freedom were accepted by close followers as being, essentially, Tantric in nature and ultimately leading to the Enlightenment. For instance, J. Hayward writes: "This is a little ironic, perhaps, in that while these other teachers have continued to propagate the traditional Tibetan Buddhist forms and styles of teaching. . . . Rinpoche abandoned all that in order to be able to make a direct and true relationship with his students, for which reason Rinpoche was first scorned and dismissed by both Tibetan and other Buddhists. Yet it was Rinpoche who first created strong and firm organizations, and new forms that carry the fresh wakefulness of the Dharma. Later, this was acknowledged and often emulated by other Tibetan teachers with growing communities in the West" (Hayward, 15).[6]

In 1970, Trungpa Rinpoche married one of his English students, Diana Judith Pybus.[7] The same year, the couple moved to the United States. Trungpa's activities dedicated to the spread of the Buddhist Dharma in the United States have been even more prolific and exuberant than in the UK. In just a few years after his arrival, between 1970 and 1975, he established the Tibetan Buddhist Meditation and Study Center in Vermont (currently known as Karme Choling Center); started a Buddhist community, "Karma Dzong," in Boulder, Colorado; founded Shambala Mountain Center in Fort Collins, Colorado (currently known as Rocky Mountain Dharma Center); initiated the Maitri Therapeutic Program; organized the Milarepa Film Workshop; founded the Mudra Theater Group; and incorporated Vajradhatu, which later became the International Association of Buddhist Meditation and Study (currently known as the Shambala International). Additionally, he established "Dorje Khyung Dzong," a retreat facility in southern Colorado; and incorporated Nalanda Foundation—a non-sectarian and non-profit educational organization dedicated to teaching Buddhist-inspired fields in psychology, general education, and art (this foundation became the beginning of the Naropa Institute which later turned into the Naropa University).

Through the 1970s and 80s, he dedicated much of his time to stimulating inter-faith dialogue. Conferences were conducted regularly at the Naropa Foundation and Institute during which philosophical and moral positions of Catholicism, Sufism, Hinduism, and Judaism were discussed, and whose participants included the most influential figures in contemporary spiritual life: Mother Tessa Bielecki, co-founder and abbess of the Spiritual Life Institute, a modern Carmelite community; Fr. Thomas Hopko, Orthodox priest and Dean of St. Vladimir's Orthodox Theological Seminary; Fr. Thomas Keating, a Trappist monk and architect of the Centering Prayer; Eido-roshi, Japanese Rinzai Zen Master; and the fourteenth Dalai Lama of Tibet.

He sponsored the Dalai Lama's participation in the Buddhist-Christian Conference in Boulder and facilitated visits by prominent Tibetan masters who had never before visited the United States or any other Western country. Specifically, he hosted, in 1974, the head of the Karmapa Kagyu lineage and the sixteenth Gyalwang Karmapa; in 1976, he invited Dilgo Khyentse Rinpoche, a revered scholar of the Nyingma lineage; and in 1975, he founded the Nalanda Translation Committee to which he invited several scholars from India and Tibet who dedicated themselves to translating Buddhist scriptures from Tibetan to English. Among other accomplishments during this phase of his life, the founding of the Alaya Preschool in Boulder must be mentioned,[8] as well as the establishment of the "Shambala Training"—a program open for all audiences (including Christian) that promotes a secular approach to meditation.

Beginning in 1982, the emphasis of his teaching activities moved from the United States to Canada, where he established the Karma Kagyu Monastery in Cape Breton, Nova Scotia, for students wishing to practice traditional monastic discipline.[9] He spent a year-long retreat in Mill Village (Nova Scotia), and in 1986, moved his home and the international headquarters of the Vajradhatu Foundation to Halifax. It was in Halifax that he died shortly after. He was cremated in the United States at the very first Buddhist center he had established there—Karme Choling in Vermont. His remains were interred in a chorten (stupa) placed near the Red Feather Lakes in Colorado. His reincarnation was recognized in 1987—a little boy born in Tibet named Chokyi Sengay.

INSTITUTIONAL HISTORY AND ACADEMIC
PROGRAMS OF THE NAROPA UNIVERSITY

Institutional history of Naropa University (NU) begins with the Naropa Institute, founded by Chogyam Trungpa (Trungpa Rinpoche) in 1974 for the purpose of studying and practicing liberal, visual, and performance arts by using Buddhist models of interconnectedness, mindfulness, meditation, and self-reflection. According to his vision, the Institute was supposed to be Buddhist-inspired, but secular in nature. He envisioned an institution involved in meditative and contemplative practices based not only in Buddhism, but in spiritual knowledge and practical education cultivated in other religions, such as Sufism, Hinduism, Judaism, and Mystical Christianity. Quoting Naropa's President Emeritus, Thomas Coburn, "The basic idea was an institute that would create an interface, a dialogue between Buddhism and the highest intellectual culture of the West. . . . If people from different traditions challenged and compared their approaches, they could go beyond conceptual mind to new perspectives, and express what they have learned in fresh ways because they are in dialogue with something different" (Coburn 2007a, 127).

But in the beginning, this was just a summer institute, and not many people who participated in it thought it would last beyond that summer of 1974. Two of Rinpoche's students, John Baker and Marvin Casper, must be particularly credited for the success of the Naropa Summer Institute. They rented a canyon outside of Boulder and raised enough money to fund the event. Everything was arranged frugally through reliance on locally available resources; for instance, an old bus garage became a classroom after it was painted and carpeted.[10] Although five hundred students were expected to enroll, two thousand people took classes that summer. The powerful experience of personal transformation which all the participants felt in the five-week semester convinced them that this educational experiment must continue. Students and professors alike felt they had been given a mission expressed in the inaugural speech of Chogyam Trungpa. He compared Western education to a sophisticated kitchen-stove capable of many technological functions but whose pilot-flame had gone extinct. He convinced his listeners that current American education, although offering information on many different subjects, had lost the flame of wisdom and no longer inspired teachers and students. The Naropa's mission was to bring back a genuine passion for learning and teaching.[11]

Original success, in which the Trungpa's ideas were accepted, did not bring the necessary financial support. NU struggled financially during its first years for it simply could not attract enough students to sustain the budget. Faculty members who took positions during the late 1970s suffered serious losses in salary, especially as compared to those universities from which they had transferred to Naropa. Unless they had a spouse with sufficient income, they had to work at other jobs just to earn enough money to pay their living expenses. Despite the hardships, the Naropa faculty strongly believed in the new model of education. This was what kept them going without adequate pay. Their greatest satisfaction lay in witnessing the creation of a completely new atmosphere for higher learning. In particular, in a world divided by racial, ethnic, and religious hatred, their university was becoming a place for cultural dialogue and peace, where students and professors of different nationalities and religious affiliations socialized and openly talked to each other; they worked together to create an open-minded and cross-cultural curriculum in liberal arts that had never before existed in America. They used spiritual, holistic, and contemplative teaching methods, and students became inspired by the true love of learning instead of a single desire for a well-paying job.[12]

Despite sacrifices made by faculty and administration alike, NU found itself on the brink of financial collapse in 1981, when the university had no other option but to close its operations. A very generous gift from an anonymous (at the time) donor allowed it to remain open. One million dollars was given to the university by one of its former students. The same donor assisted in purchasing a piece of land along Arapaho Avenue where the main campus of NU (Lincoln Campus) has been developed. With this gift, Naropa's financial woes subsided. A solid endowment was created and money spent frugally over the next decade.

This process of financial stabilization was followed, in 1986, by full accreditation from the North Central Association of Colleges and Schools, making NU the first Buddhist-inspired institution of higher learning to receive such an accreditation. Soon after that, in 1991, NU absorbed Boulder Graduate School and developed its second campus—Paramita Campus— where graduate programs in the field of psychology are now offered.

Creative inspirations continued in the following years and, in 2003, a completely new campus—Nalanda Campus—opened which is now fully integrated with the other two campuses (*Newsletter of Naropa University*, 8). Named after the oldest Buddhist university in India, the Nalanda campus opened with a specific purpose—to house art programs. John Cobb, then president of NU, emphasized unique pedagogical approaches to arts and performance at NU and of the importance of arts-programs for infusing creative life into the entire university's community. Thomas Coburn, who followed him as NU president, explained in full why arts are such an important element of the Naropa style of education, "Like meditation, the arts expand our mundane consciousness, opening our limited conventional perspectives to larger possibilities. They offer new ways of thinking, feeling, and experiencing both the world and ourselves" (Coburn 2007b).

Since the 1970s, the number of undergraduate students at NU has grown from thirty to nearly nine hundred. The number of permanent faculty grew from the original ten instructors to more than seventy. In the process, serious emphasis was put on developing graduate programs. At present, NU offers the following degrees:

Undergraduate:

- contemplative psychology
- early childhood education
- environmental studies
- interdisciplinary studies
- music
- peace studies
- performance
- religious studies
- traditional Eastern arts
- visual arts
- writing and literature

Graduate:

- art therapy
- body psychotherapy
- contemplative education
- contemplative psychotherapy
- counseling psychology
- dance/movement therapy
- divinity
- ecopsychology
- environmental leadership
- religious studies
- religious studies with language
- theater: contemporary performance
- wilderness therapy
- writings and poetics

One of the most distinguished programs at NU is Contemplative Education. Prof. Richard Brown, who founded in 1990 the Department of Contemplative Education at NU, now serves as a consultant with the Garrison Institute's Initiative on Contemplation and Education; former president, Thomas Co-burn, established the Center for the Advancement of Contemplative Educa-tion, a national institution promoting contemplative education in American colleges and universities; while yet another distinguished citizen of NU, Prof. Simmer-Brown, assembled *Meditation and the Classroom*, a pioneering collective monograph discussing academic and personal benefits of contemplative teaching and learning.

Contemplative methods at NU are employed across the curriculum. They take on many different forms, and students can choose the contemplative practice they pursue. Choices include centering prayer, yoga, Jewish meditation, Taich'i, Shamatha, Aikido, Brush-Calligraphy, and Ikebana. A set of academic requirements and grading procedures have been purposely developed for those courses in which contemplative learning plays a large role and bears on the final grade. Quoting from *Meditation and the Classroom*, "we are not introducing religious practices; we are developing new teaching pedagogies. We are not creating little Buddhists, Hassidis, Sufis, Daoists, or Trappists. We are returning to the roots of liberal education in the West. These roots are grounded in the development of depth and wholeness synchronized with intellectual rigor . . . Contemplative pedagogies have the potential to return the transformative qualities to our educational endeavors" (Simmer-Brown and Grace, 110).

Based on Richard Brown's explanation, it is not the practice of meditation, yoga, Ikebana, or Taich'i that is graded, but the ways in which students draw on their own insights obtained through such practices. The insight must include more than merely a reaction to the exercise; it must reach levels of psychological and intellectual sophistication showing that the "first-person" investigation of the subject has been activated and has progressed over the time of the course. Rubrics for grading include such categories as "comprehension," "integration," "development of initial observations," and "re-evaluation of the original observations upon a deeper contemplation."

When in 2003, the first annual Naropa Alumni Reunion was held, an alumna, Jill Goldwarg, expressed everyone's appreciation of the contemplative training at Naropa by saying, "In revisiting my place of education, I value it even more now because I have seen how it works in my life and know that in the face of life's real challenges, I am successful not by what I do, but by who I am. That kind of education is invaluable" (Goldwarg).

Naropa's leading role in promoting contemplative education nation-wide is well-recognized, as faculty from other universities who wish to use similar methods are in constant dialogue with Naropa faculty and regularly come here to be trained (Coburn, Grace, Klein, et al.). Closely related to Naropa's contemplative pedagogy is its emphasis on studying and practicing the arts. Although in many national institutions of higher learning art programs suffer from financial cuts and are generally under-appreciated, here, at this university, faculty and students alike understand that they cannot be fully human unless they are exposed to the beauty of the human artistic expressions and are capable of discovering the "artist" within their own psyche. Artistic approach to life, I was told, drives inspiration in the daily tasks which, otherwise, tend to become mechanical and robot-like.

At NU, visual art expressions are found everywhere: on Lincoln campus, rock and flower arrangements are being regularly created in and outside the classrooms; on Paramita campus, art exhibits by students practicing art therapy are a regular and welcome occurrence; and Nalanda campus hosts most art classes and exhibitions which always bustle with students' and visitors' activities.

Naropa Community Art Studio is a unique extension of this "personal cultivation through arts" to a larger group of people. The studio offers a place for both university and city of Boulder communities to gather and create together. Equal access to non-university members is emphasized, especially for those people who have been culturally marginalized and are unlikely to have previous experience with the arts. This Naropa Community Art Studio is managed by the Art Therapy faculty, alumni, and graduates who organize the space in many different ways, offering their services as art mentors. "Unity in diversity, the birthright to pursue creative expression, and the capacity of visual arts to contain and communicate the full range of human experiences compose the essence of the Studio's mission and focus" (*Naropa University Academic Catalog*, 2010–2011, 27–28).

The importance of self-reflection and self-cultivation through practices of visualization and public performance are at the heart and center of Naropa's redesigned BFA in Performance. Drawing from the Shamabala Buddhist concept of a "warrior artist," the program blends the artistic process with contemplative meditative practices. It combines voice skills with movement and dance instructions in a conservatory-style of learning and requires three eight-hour a day, three days a week, participation. "Every day of class is intense," says former student, Earl Kim. "You are faced with an imaginary mirror and are challenged to really, truly find yourself, then let it shine out . . . Through every technique explored—viewpoints, Feldenkrais, Grotowsky, etc.—we learn to question everything, especially ourselves" (Johnson).

BFA Ensemble Training Modules are some of the most integrated and innovative ways of training new artists and performers in the United States. According to the *Catalog*, "Each module is progressive interdisciplinary sequence in dance, acting, and voice applicable to creating original work and includes training in exercises and techniques developed during the past 15 years of performance as well as strong elements of research. Each module represents approximately 80 hours of voice training and processes such as Estill, Roy Hart, and Linklater method; 80 hours of dance training in forms inspired by artists of the postmodern movement and beyond, with courses in Contemporary Dance Technique, Contact Improvisation, Body/Mind entering, Spontaneous Composition and World Forms; and 100 (or more) hours in actor training and devised work, including work in Physical Acting Grotow-ski, Viewpoints, Script/Text Analysis, Self-scripting and Project Develop-ment. Across all disciplines, students are encouraged to discover their own creative process, participate in ensample creation, direct elements of their own training, consciously choose techniques, and develop a contemplative approach to the creative process" (*Catalog 2010–2011*, 109).

NU is world-famous not only for its art and performance education, but also for its literature and writing programs taught through the Jack Kerouac School of Disembodied Poetics (JKS). Rinpoche's fame as a life-transform-ing spiritual guru attracted to him some of the best poets and writers of the 1970s and 1980s. Among many books dedicated to this aspect of Naropa's history, Anne Waldman's and Marilyn Webb's edited volumes on the history of JKS provide thorough and well documented material on all aspects of the school's history and its most celebrated teachers and students, true giants of American literature such as Alan Ginsberg, Anne Waldman, John Cage, and Diane de Prima, while the more recent Kashner's *When I Was Cool: My Life at Jack Kerouac School* gives us a colorful, humorous, and detailed picture of the era when the school was just in its initial phase. Many outstanding American writers and poets have contributed to the Kerouac School's history and helped develop its unique creative environment. Anne Waldman who, together with Alan Ginsberg, founded JKS in 1974 is still affiliated with NU.[13]

Today's Jack Kerouac School of Disembodied Poetics emphasizes inno-vative approaches to literary arts. It problematizes genre distinctions while helping students cultivate contemplative and experimental approaches to writing. Each year, the school invites more than sixty guest faculty to the internationally renowned summer writing program, a four-week colloquium of workshops, lectures, and readings. These distinguished features of the summer program foster an intensely creative environment for students who develop writing projects in a conversation with the community of writers.

The regular curriculum of JKS includes courses in innovative prose, poet-ry, and cross-genre forms, as well as professional development in teaching and publishing. Along with writing, students partake in contemplative and somatic practices to develop their own integrative creative processes. Under-graduate training consists of core writing seminars and a BA in creative writing and literature; at the graduate level, residential MFA in creative writing and poetics, and summer writing programs are offered.

Interviews conducted with the JKS graduates revealed that students espe-cially value a contemplative approach to learning about, and practicing, writ-ing. In the classroom, students become writers, thinkers, meditators, observ-ers, teachers, and facilitators of others' creative-writing processes. Students particularly praised the relationship they were able to create with their in-structors, as well as the opportunity given to them to create a relationship with one's own inner, individual writer. Many expressed the notion that the freedom to explore what is literature and writing are all about is far greater at NU than at any other college or university where they had studied before. Some graduates in the NU writing programs admitted to being professional publishers who (as a part of their job) have come across published and submitted works by JKS graduates. According to their confession, they had encountered such magnificent, never encountered before experiential prose and poetry in these writings that they felt compelled to enroll at JKS. Using the words of one of these students, at JKS, the classroom becomes a laboratory, where understanding and becoming mindful of every word, every sentence, and every possible connection between emotions, thoughts, and verbal expressions, are being explored. The summary of the training is teaching a creative-writing workshop in one self-chosen community in Boulder. So many students I have talked with have expressed their appreciation of "the aura of excitement, of the mystery, of falling in love with the word, of realizing that one can do so much with the Word in order to change the world for the better."

This brief overview of NU academic programs would be incomplete without saying a few words about another outstanding program which attracts students from all over the country—a Graduate School in Psychology.[14] According to the catalog, this program is grounded in mindfulness/awareness training and students pursue didactic and experiential coursework in art therapy and transpersonal counseling psychology along with various opportunities to practice in the field. The program is approved by the American Art Therapy Association and accredited, in 1988, by the Higher Learning Commission of the North Central Association of Colleges and Schools.

Because Buddhism has been historically centered on issues of human wellbeing and mental hygiene (Blows; de Silva; Kwee), it is not surprising that, at all four Buddhist universities, programs based in Buddhist psychology are well developed. NU offers more degrees in the fields of psychology, human development, and mental counseling than other Buddhist universities. At the undergraduate level, degrees are granted in contemplative psychology and early childhood education. These bachelor's degrees are well-recognized, practically guaranteeing professional placement right after graduation. Graduate degrees (MA) offer a great variety of pursuits in psychotherapy, including contemplative psychology, counseling psychology, art therapy, body psychotherapy, dance/movement therapy, and ecopsychology. Thirty-four percent of the graduate population at NU find jobs through graduation from these programs and thereafter provide counseling and mental health services to Americans.

STUDENTS AT THE NAROPA UNIVERSITY

NU Career Services and Alumni Relations have being collecting, for several years, data about its graduates and their post-graduation activities. The most recent report indicates that 94 percent of undergraduates and 90 percent of the graduates are working and/or attending graduate and professional schools; while only 6 percent of the undergraduates and 10 percent of the graduates are still seeking their next position in life. Nearly 60 percent of the undergraduates who are employed indicate that their positions are related to their majors; 67 percent of the graduates report similar connections between the chosen career of their life and the discipline they pursued at NU.

I interviewed twelve undergraduate students who I met on NU campuses, asking them the same question, "What do you want to learn at this university?" Their answers, in some way, spoke of their "huge commitment to changing the world for the better." Some specific ways in which they planned to make the world a better place included 1) merging information technology with wisdom, 2) changing our consumption culture, 3) teaching Americans how to see the world as a beautiful place by bringing more art and music into our communities, 4) finding more connections between mind and body in every form of our daily activity, and 5) making people more aware of what they are doing to themselves and others.

It is no wonder, therefore, that when we look at the career paths typically chosen by NU alumni, we see careers mainly in health/healing/retreats, education/training, and environmental/natural resources. A good number of the graduates, nearly 34 percent, choose counseling and mental health careers; while others found successful employment in arts and communication, business administration, computers and technology, human services, and publishing and writing.

In the winter of 2013, I conducted an extensive interview with Holly Hisamoto who had recently received her undergraduate degree from NU. My first question to her was about the value of the Buddhist-based education. This is what she said:

> I wanted education that would change my whole life for the better and teach me how to help other people. I did not want to jump through the hoops and receive good grades just for the sake of it. I strongly believe that good education must change student's life for the better. So, for me, this was *the whole person education* that I value most.

My second question to Holly was: "How did the Buddhist-based education prepare you for your life outside the university?"

In answering this question, she chose to speak of the training she had received at the Naropa, called "Three Types of Knowledge," or "Three Prajnas." She explained: "First, my knowledge comes from 'Hearing;' that is, when I simply listen to people relating to me their problems. In this type of knowledge, I make no decisions and create no emotional or intellectual responses to what I hear. I simply absorb everything that is there, in the situation. Then, I go into a phase of knowledge, called 'Contemplating,' when I ponder all causes and consequences involved in the situation. I contemplate possible outcomes, as well as the ways in which I can affect lives of the people involved in the situation. The third level of knowledge is acquired through 'Integrating.' It is then, that I understand—I am a part of the solution just as much as I am a part of the problem. Here, I take personal moral responsibility for the whole issue, no matter what decision (or no decision) will be made by me, or someone else. Integrating involves a realization that I have my own emotional responses to the various aspects of the situation and dealing with them in a peaceful way. This keeps me grounded and helps avoid personal suffering as I take care of people with kindness and patience."

Holly explained that her first job after graduation was with the Head-Start program for children with low economic status. She explained,

> I used my Early Childhood Education degree from Naropa University to get this job, and it was there, that I realized how well prepared I was for this job! I realized—I have patience, I have compassion, and I know how to stay calm by taking regular breaks and practicing meditation!

I also asked Holly: "What principles of the Buddhist-based pedagogy have been proven most valuable in your post-graduate and professional life?"

She replied that the education she received at NU had shaped her entire life, including the way she approaches new knowledge and new information. She said,

> Even though my mind has been constantly enlarged and developed with the new information, it was at Naropa that I learned how to receive new information with humility. I learned how to let go of my ego in the process of learning and avoid personal projections, expectations, and assumptions of any kind. I would describe a Buddhist way of receiving information as a Yin-Yang process. On one hand, you are encouraged to learn and receive as much as you can. But on the other, you are trained to let go of all "ego-grasping." No self-aggrandizement and no self-deprecation either. In the end, I think, this helped me develop a mind that is opened and curious, and my ego no longer interferes with the process of learning.
>
> Another important pedagogical principle," she added, "is to involve the awareness of a student's whole body in the process of learning. We are not robots. We are not just our heads floating in empty spaces! We have physical bodies and emotional reactions, which influence how we perceive information and what we do with it. Through a series of exercises, such as Taich'i, Meditation, and Centering Prayer, students at Naropa learn to observe their personal

reactions to different thoughts and emotions. They become aware of anger, frustration, depression, anxiety, pride, and other emotion rising in response to a specific learning process. This was very helpful to me as a student, because it prevented me from burning out and feeling unhappy and depressed. It is helpful now at my workplace because I recognize people's emotional responses involved in the mental processes.

My final question to Holly was about the use of her education at the present. Here, I found out that she is a Chaplain Resident at the Legacy Emanuel Medical Center in Portland, OR, where she works with the patients struggling with PTSD, life-threatening diseases, and potential death. She has to take care of their relatives dealing with grief and fear of losing loved ones. Without the Buddhist-inspired education, she said, she would not be able to work with so much human trauma, yet remain grounded and focused. She added that her training had opened her to the people's religious diversity and helped adopt pluralistic views in all her daily activities.

NOTES

1. I had my first encounter with the Naropa campus in 2010. In 2011, I found a passage in *Meditation and the Classroom* which explained a deeper meaning of what I had observed: "How can mindfulness-awareness practice be useful in developing contemplative pedagogy? . . . One way to begin this transition is to bring tangible reminders of mindfulness practice . . . A particular object placed on our desks or somewhere . . . can serve as a reminder of mindfulness . . . a small piece of driftwood or a stone collected on a retreat could serve as a reminder to notice, let go, and wake up to present moment" (Simmer-Brown and Grace, 77).

2. The story is remarkably similar to the story about the Buddha's conception. Buddha was conceived after his mother saw in her dream that a snow-white, glowing with the bright light, six-tusked elephant had entered into her womb.

3. The Nyingma is considered to be the oldest. It is known for its strong emphasis on esoteric, Tantric, aspects of learning and lineage. Sakya teaches that the path to nirvana and nirvana itself cannot be distinguished and emphasizes the need for an experienced guru to attain this realization. The Kagyu is known for its use of the "mahamudra," "the great seal," which, when passed to a student, reveals the essential nature of reality, that is a unity of luminosity and emptiness. It involves a direct and sudden insight into the innate luminosity and emptiness of existence which bring liberation from ignorance and afflictive emotion. And the Geluk places greater emphasis on studying scriptures and practicing traditional monastic discipline than the other three schools. The fourteenth Dalai Lama is of the Geluk School. For more on Tibetan schools of Buddhism, see Powers and Lopez.

4. An ongoing publicly supported project collects oral history about Trungpa Rinpoche. When completed, it will include all stories and memories by his students and other people who knew him. This project is strikingly reminiscent of how the Buddhist canon, Tripitaka, was put together after the Buddha's death by his disciples at the First Buddhist Council.

5. According to others, the decision to do so was slowly developing over a period of time.

6. I interviewed Rita Gross in 2012, asking her opinion on this subject. She answered that, by setting aside strict monastic behavior, "Rinpoche gave people a chance to pursue their own spiritual growth and inner enrichment." Charles Carreon and Peter Bishop discussed the problems of authoritarianism in Tibetan and American Buddhism; their discussion helps understand the intention behind Trungpa's unorthodox behavior. He himself wrote in *Transcending Madness* and *You Might be Tired of the Seat That You Deserve* about limiting effects religious orthodoxy is having on the evolution of human consciousness.

7. She became later known as Diana Mukpo. The story of her marriage to Rinpoche is in Mukpo. Also see Silberman for her interview given to the *Shambala Sun*.

8. The preschool successfully functions to this day. Its pedagogy is consistent with Trungpa Rinpoche's vision for wisdom-inspired education. Its website reads, "The Alaya preschool arises out of compassion and caring for others. . . . Within [the preschool's] homelike and nurturing environment, children are able to observe and participate in simple basic living activities: relationships, helping, sharing, reading and telling stories, preparing food, cleaning up, caring for plants and animals, and learning through play. The development of the classroom as a community is an important part of our program." Historical connections to Trungpa Rinpoche's methodology are emphasized through a quote from his inaugural speech (1978): "'Alaya' is a Sanskrit word. It means 'storehouse,' and 'origin.' It means that big things are happening, primordial things taking place. And that is what we're trying to do." Chogyam Trungpa also founded the Shambala School (first through twelfth grades) in Halifax, Nova Scotia. This makes him rather similar to Master Xuan Hua, the founder of the "Instilling Goodness" elementary and "Developing Virtue" secondary schools in the City of Ten Thousand Buddhas. (About these schools, see chapter two of this book.)

9. Canada was a familiar place for Rinpoche and his wife. On the way to the United States, they stopped in Canada because of Diana's visa problems. According to her, the couple lived frugally in an old studio apartment in the university district of Montreal until American students who studied with Rinpoche in Samye Ling in the UK came to help them financially; they also gave him the idea to start a Buddhist practice center in Vermont (Silberman).

10. From the interview with the Naropa faculty who taught in the original Naropa Summer Institute.

11. Information received in the interview with NU Professor, Judith Simmer-Brown.

12. Information obtained through private interviews with NU facutly.

13. Ginsberg was close friend and student of Rinpoche and lived in Boulder for several years; he played a most active role in the creation of this school, and this is why rich archive materials about Ginsberg's years in Boulder are kept in the main library on the Lincoln campus. The library is named after Ginsberg. Overall, the JKS's history is covered far better than any other program at NU. Along with the above mentioned sources, one can consult official JKS blog and audio archives in Alan Ginsberg's library.

14. Marvin Casper, who had helped organize the Naropa Summer Institute in 1974, also became a leader in restructuring the original psychology program at Naropa.

REFERENCES FOR CHAPTER THREE

Blows, M. 1993. *Towards the Whole Person: Integrating Eastern and Western Approaches to Body-Mind Skills*. Kenthurst NSW: Linking Publications.

Coburn, Thomas. 2007a. "The Arts and the 'In-between' Spaces," *Naropa Magazine*, spring issue: 1.

———. 2007b. "Naropa University: Reflecting the Interplay of Discipline and Delight," *Bodhi Magazine*, v. 9: 126–29.

Coburn, Thomas, Fran Grace, Anne Klein et al. 2011. "Contemplative Pedagogy: Frequently Asked Questions," *Teaching Theology and Religion*, v. 14, issue 2: 167–74.

Coleman, James. 2000. *The New Buddhism: The Western Transformation of an Ancient Tradition*. New York: Oxford University Press.

Dass, Ram. 1971. *Be Here Now*. Taos, NM: Lama Foundation.

De Silva, Padmal. 2000. "Buddhism and Psychotherapy," *Hsi Lai Journal of Humanistic Buddhism* 1: 169–81.

Goldwarg, Jill. 2003. "Revisiting," *Newsletter of Naropa University*, July 2003:12.

Hayward, Jeremy. 2008. *Warrior-King of Shamabala: Remembering Chogyam Trungpa*. Boston: Wisdom Publications.

History of Naropa. 2013. http://www.naropa.edu/about-naropa/history

Johnson, Owen. 2009. "Earth Day Celebration Signals Completion of Naropa Green House." *Naropa Magazine*, spring issue: 2–3.

Kwee, M. G. 1990. *Psychotherapy, Meditation and Health*. London: East-West Publications.

Lopez, Donald. 1997. (ed.) *Religions of Tibet in Practice*. Princeton, NJ: Princeton University Press.

Midal, Fabrice. 2004. *Chogyam Trungpa: His Life and Vision*. Boston: Shamabala Publication.

Mukpo, Diana. 2006. *Dragon Thunder: My Life with Chogyam Trungpa*. Boston: Shamabala Publication.

Naropa University. 2010. *Naropa University Academic Catalog*, 2010–2011.

———. 2003. *Newsletter of Naropa University*.

Paine, Jeffrey. 2004. *Re-Enchantment: Tibetan Buddhism comes to the West*, 1st Edition. New York: W. W. Norton & Company.

Powers, John. 1995. *Introduction to Tibetan Buddhism*. Ithaca, NY: Snow Lion Publications.

Silberman, Steve. 2006. "Married to the Guru," *Shambala Sun*, November 2006: 1–6.

Simmer-Brown, Judith. 2009. "The Question is the Answer: Naropa University's Contemplative Pedagogy," *Religion and Education*, summer issue.

Simmer-Brown, Judith, and Fran Grace. 2011. *Meditation and the Classroom: Contemplative Pedagogy for Religious Studies*. New York: State University of New York Press.

Trungpa, Chogyam. 2000. *Born in Tibet*. Boston: Shamabala Publications.

———. 2004. *The Collected Works of Chogyam Trungpa*, 8 vols. Boston: Shamabala Publications.

———. 2000b. *Journey without Goal*. Boston: Shamabala Publications.

Chapter Four

Soka University of America

FIRST ENCOUNTER

I wrote in previous chapters dedicated to three other Buddhist universities that the sense of beauty and harmony created on their campuses is accomplished through the use of simple and inexpensive means. As simple, indeed, as a stack of balanced rocks on a rough wooden surface of a table standing in front of the main hall at the Naropa campus; or as inexpensive as feeding a dozen peacocks roaming freely around the Dharma Realm University campus. In this respect, Soka University of America is different. I will explain later how grandiose and costly the structures we encounter are consistent with the Soka Gakkai principles upon which this university is built, but right now, I must describe my first encounter with the campus.

The moment I arrived, I saw a breathtakingly beautiful, large lake with a fountain at each end. The turquoise-blue space of water, with the fountains sending shimmering silver strings into a quiet fragrant morning, looked as if they have just been borrowed from a fairytale. I could not take my eyes away, although I was almost late for my appointment. A moment later, I saw a palace with a high-dome standing by the side of the lake. Its classical façade reminded me vividly of magnificent European castles, chateaus, and cathedrals. I discovered soon enough that the palace with the dome is "Founders Hall" and it honors people from around the world who have contributed to the construction of the campus. Thousands of donors' names have been engraved on the walls inside the round vestibule, where I stepped in search of the room indicated in my appointment. The floor in the round vestibule depicted a map of the world, and in a circular shape around it, thirty national flags stood, reminding us of the countries from which the donors have come.

No matter where I walked on campus after that, I could always see the dome of the Founders Hall. It is so bright that it can be spotted from miles away. Its color looks like gold, but it isn't; it is made of copper. Three thousand seven hundred and fifty pounds of copper were used in the double-dome construction of Founders Hall modeled after the famous Florence Cathedral in Italy. And at the same time, two thousand and eight hundred tons of famous travertine stone were used to build this hall and other buildings on campus. The travertine stone was purposely chosen because of its historical significance—it is a rare stone found in Italy, which was used for building Rome's Coliseum.

Inside Founders Hall, adjacent to the round vestibule, there are admissions, student recruitment, registrar, and human resources offices. On the second floor, the art gallery is open every weekday; admission is free.

The lake I saw on the morning of my arrival is known as "Peace Lake." With a bio-filter system and twin fountains keeping the water clean, Peace Lake is a backup reservoir for the campus's water needs and a pump-station for fire protection. Stone walkways divide it into three parts: Passion, Victory, and Wisdom. These walkways between the lake's segments are barely visible from a distance, yet they are comfortable for people to walk on. When I saw a mother and two children on the walkway between the "Victory" and "Wisdom," they looked exactly as if they were walking on water.

LIFE OF DAISAKU IKEDA,
FOUNDER OF THE SOKA UNIVERSITY OF AMERICA

Unlike the founders of the three other Buddhist-inspired universities, the founder of Soka University of America (SUA), Mr. Ikeda Daisaku, is not a member of the Buddhist clergy, nor has he ever received monastic training of any kind. He is a lay Buddhist and the founder of one of the largest lay Buddhist organizations—Soka Gakkai International (SGI)—that included nearly ten million members according to the 2013 census.[1] It can be also said that he is one of the most influential Buddhist leaders alive because the Nichiren Buddhism—a particular school upon which the Soka Gakkai International was founded—is now practiced in more than 192 countries and territories.

According to the official biography posted on the SGI site, Daisaku Ikeda was born in 1928 in Tokyo. He was the fifth of eight children in a family of seaweed farmers. As a child, he suffered from tuberculosis and doctors predicted that he would not live beyond 30 years of age; nonetheless, he enjoyed a relatively healthy and very fruitful life and is still alive today.

In childhood, he fell on difficult times when Japan's militaristic regime was preparing the nation for World War II allied with Nazi Germany. Three of his brothers were drafted and injured, and one brother was killed during the war. His brothers' descriptions of the war's atrocities left a deep impression on his heart and mind. He had a personal experience with it, too—the Ikeda's home was destroyed in the firebombing of Tokyo when 100,000 Japanese were killed.

Most likely, the terrifying effects of the war made Daisaku Ikeda interested in Buddhist philosophy and the teachings of Nichiren.[2] He developed an admiration for, and became a close disciple of, Mr. Josei Toda (1900–1958), who was the second president of the Soka Gakkai of Japan.[3] Mr. Toda opposed the policies of the wartime government and promoted human dignity and liberty which, for him, were merely a logical conclusion of his acceptance of Nichiren's position seeing all people as equal, endowed with the same potential for liberation from suffering through their Buddha-nature. For his views he suffered persecution and a two-year imprisonment.

Mr. Daisaku met Mr. Toda soon after Toda was released from the prison, and the two of them became inseparable. Toda educated young Daisaku in world literature and history, as well as in chemistry, physics, law, and political science. Daisaku officially joined the Soka Gakkai of Japan in 1947 while Toda still was its president. A decade after his beloved teacher passed away, Ikeda Daisaku succeeded him as the third Soka Gakkai president. Since then, he has committed himself to spreading Mr. Toda's teachings throughout Japan and the global community.

One of the first initiatives he undertook involved short trips abroad in order to encourage those Soka members who lived outside of Japan. In the United States and in other countries he visited, he tried to establish organizational structures which would encourage and facilitate more frequent interaction between the members. Within his first years as president, he traveled to North and South America, Europe, Asia, Middle East, and Oceania, laying foundations for the overseas organizations. Simultaneously, he started building research and cultural institutions dedicated to promoting world peace. The most famous of these institutions founded during the early years of presidency are the Institute of Oriental philosophy (1962) and the Min-on Concert Association (1963). These were followed by the Tokyo Fuji Art Museum (1983); The Ikeda Center for Peace, Learning, and Dialogue (1993); and the Toda Institute for Global Peace and Policy Research (1996).

His world-peace activities reached a new level in 1975 after the establishment of the Soka Gakkai International. In January of that year, representatives from 51 countries gathered on the island of Guam to form an international forum for peace. The site of some of the bloodiest fighting during World War II had been symbolically chosen to expand the Japanese organization Soka Gakkai to a new international organization—Soka Gakkai International (SGI). Soka Gakkai International has quickly developed into a global network promoting peace, culture, and education in the societies participating in SGI chapters by organizing large-scale international public exhibitions on current human problems and calling public attention to such urgent issues as control of nuclear power, sustainable economic development, and protection of human rights.

It was during those years that Mr. Ikeda became known for his international attempts at normalizing Sino-Japanese diplomatic relations. On September 8, 1968, he addressed 20,000 SGI members, outlining specific steps toward achieving better relationships between his country and the People's Republic of China. At that time, the PRC was perceived as an enemy nation by many Japanese and still isolated within the international community. Daisaku Ikeda's proposal caught the attention of those who were interested in restoring relations between the two countries. The era was filled with deep tensions between the superpowers threatening nuclear annihilation. During 1974–75, Mr. Ikeda visited the PRC, the USSR, and the United States, meeting with Soviet Premier Aleksey Kosygin, U.S. Secretary of State Henry Kissinger, and Chinese Premier Zhou Enlai, in an effort to break the deadlock and open channels of communication, so as to prevent the outbreak of nuclear war.

One of the hallmarks of Ikeda's "Peace Philosophy" has been his commitment to international dialogues. He met and exchanged views with many representatives of cultural, political, educational, and artistic fields. These meetings led to publications of many collaborative dialogues with other world-peace leaders, including Abdurrahman Wahid (1940–2009), the founder of the National Awakening Party and first democratically elected president of Indonesia; Harvey J. Cox (1922–), a leading United States theologian and Hollis Research Professor at the Harvard Divinity School; Hazel Henderson (1933–), famous author of several futuristic books, including *Beyond Globalization*, *Planetary Citizenship*, and *Ethical Markets*; Jin Yong (1924–), Chinese novelist and founder of the Hong Kong daily *Ming Pao*; and Mikhail Gorbachev (1931–), the former General Secretary of the Communist Part of the Soviet Union, among others.

Since 1983, Mr. Ikeda has been writing world peace proposals, which he continues to publish annually on the anniversary of the SGI—January 26. In January of 2013, he wrote a peace proposal that stressed the centrality of the dignity of life and called for a complete abolition of nuclear weapons. It called for a renewed dialogue between China and Japan and creation of an organization specifically responsible for environmental protection across East Asia. "The time has come," he wrote, "to develop more concrete models of cooperation across a range of new fields. I am convinced that it is through such sustained and determined efforts that the bonds of friendship between China and Japan will develop into something indestructible, something that will be passed down with pride from generation to generation."[4]

In the 2014 Peace Proposal, he summarized the goals of the Soka education by writing: "I would like to offer specific proposals focusing on three key areas critical to the effort to create a sustainable global society. The first relates to education with a particular focus on young people . . . I urge that targets related to education be included . . . specifically, to achieve universal access to primary and secondary education, to eliminate gender disparity at all levels and to promote education for global citizenship."[5] The other two key areas include the abolition of nuclear weapons and strengthening people's resilience all around the world. "In the broadest sense, resilience can be thought of in terms of realizing a hopeful future, rooted in people's natural desire to work together toward common goals."[6]

INSTITUTIONAL HISTORY AND ACADEMIC PROGRAMS OF THE SOKA UNIVERSITY OF AMERICA

Institutional history and academic programs at Soka University of America (SUA) are inseparable from Soka Gakkai of Japan and Soka Gakkai International.[7] The word *gakkai* means "society." *Soka* is derived from two Japanese words: *sozo* ("creation") and *kachi* ("value") and literally means "value creation." Soka education, in short, focuses on students' innate abilities and teaches them how to create beauty and value in every aspect of human life and nature. The beginning of this Soka-education is associated with the name of a Japanese teacher, Tsunesaburo Makiguchi (1871–1944).

Mr. Makiguchi was born to a poor family in Nigata, and his parents abandoned him when he was only six years old. Fortunately for him and for all of us, he was adopted by relatives and, despite tremendous challenges, managed to graduate from a school for future teachers in Hokkaido. Later, he worked as a principal in elementary schools in Tokyo.

A good analysis of Mr. Makiguchi's life and his philosophy of education is in D. Bethel's *Education for Creative Living: Ideas and Proposals of Tsunesaburo Makiguchi*, and N. Sharma's *Value Creators in Education: Japanese Educator Makiguchi and Mahatma Gandhi and Their Relevance for the Indian Education*. According to them, Makiguchi's ideas developed under the influence of John Dewey and Mahatma Gandhi. Mr. Makiguchi studied, in translations, their speeches and written works, and he became convinced that the role of a teacher must be that of a guide who empowers students and helps them take responsibility for their own learning.

In 1903, he published his first major work, *Geography of Human Life* (Jinsei Chirigaku), declaring that freedom and rights of the individual, including the right to education, are sacred and inviolable.[8] This work was followed, in 1930–1934, by four volumes of *The System of Value-Creating Pedagogy* (Soka Kyoikugaku Taikei) in which he further affirmed that education cannot be forced upon a human being but must be delivered through dialogue and personal empowerment. Through dialogue and personal empowerment, Makiguchi believed, individuals can reveal their fullest potential and create value in their own lives, as well as in the lives of their immediate communities (Kumagai, 40–43). By doing so, they can attain happiness and, simultaneously, contribute to the betterment of society. He is quoted as saying, "The aim of education is not to transfer knowledge; it is to guide the learning process, to equip learner with the methods of research. It is not the piecemeal merchandising of information; it is to enable the acquisition of the methods for learning on one's own; it is the provision of keys to unlock the vault of knowledge. Rather than encouraging students to appropriate the intellectual treasures uncovered by others, we should enable them to undertake on their own the process of discovery and invention" (Tsuji, 105).[9]

During 1913–1932, Mr. Makiguchi worked in different schools around Tokyo. This allowed him an opportunity to refine his educational theories into a practical form. He continuously emphasized (and carried this into practice) that each child must be treated with the utmost respect and care, especially, economically disadvantaged children who must be given a place at school where they can regain their human dignity. Meanwhile, Japan was preparing for World War II. Japanese national education was transformed into the Shinto religion-based ideological propaganda, declaring the emperor to be a divine being, called "kami," and the descendant of the Sun-Goddess, Amaterasu. The so-called sacred obligation to sacrifice one's life for the sake of this divine emperor, called the "Mikado," was imposed on all Japanese. [10]

By contrast, Mr. Makiguchi based his ideas on Western and Buddhist philosophy underscoring the dignity of the individual. Before and during the war, he insisted that the main goal of public schools must be to help students discover their consciousness, pursue personal fulfillment, and grow to become valuable members of the society. For his views, he was imprisoned and tortured. He died in 1944, a year before the collapse of the imperial nationalistic regime of Japan, never knowing how successful his educational program would become once a peaceful society was restored in his country.

Makiguchi's contribution to the education of children worldwide involved more than developing and practicing these liberal social goals. He left a long-lasting legacy by founding a public-supported association for teachers who were fully dedicated to promoting these goals—Soka Gakkai of Japan. One crucial aspect of the Soka Gakkai of Japan was building "value-creating" schools and kindergartens that were free and open to all children, regardless of their social and economic status. The massive scale of these operations took place during the later part of the twentieth century. In 1976, the Sapporo Soka Kindergarten was built for the children of Hokkaido who had suffered from discrimination by the Japanese government. In 1992, a Soka kindergarten opened in Hong Kong, primarily for the children of Japanese descent mistreated by other ethnic groups because of Japan's role in World War II. The school enrolled other children as well, especially if they experienced difficulty being accepted elsewhere. Beginning in 1993, Soka schools and kindergartens opened in other parts of Asia—Singapore in 1993; Kuala Lumpur, Malaysia, in 1995; and Seoul, South Korea, in 2008. Soka schools also opened in South America, in countries such as Brazil.

The history of the Soka schools and kindergartens is important because it explains one unique characteristic of the Soka University of America. It helps us understand why, during a time of economic crisis, this small private university has an operating endowment of more than 400 million dollars, while its scholarship endowment exceeds 100 million dollars. The explanation is in the Soka-education's support system.

SUA president Dr. Daniel Habuki, being of humble origin, would not have had a chance for education, were it not for the Soka institutions. When he became president, he wrote hundreds of letters to people who had attended and graduated from various Soka schools, including the Tokyo-based high school from which he graduated. Soka graduates from around the world made generous donations to the American Soka University, eventually placing it in a unique position among other colleges and universities for this is one university which does not depend on money coming from students' tuition to pay for its programs.

As a private, four-year Liberal Arts College and University, SUA ranks among the top 50 in the nation according to "Best Colleges 2014" in *U.S. News and World Report.* Yet, in the beginning, SUA was practically unknown. It opened in 1987 as a not-for-profit organization incorporated in the State of California. It was located then inside a small graduate school in Calabasas on property known to be one of the sites of the Chumash Indian ancestral burial grounds. When, within a few years of its establishment, SUA decided to expand its campus, the decision met with resistance from Californian public groups seeking to protect the ancestral site (Walker).

This is why, in 1995, the SUA administration purchased 103 acres of rough-graded property in Aliso Viejo, Orange County. It purchased land for 25 million dollars and then spent 225 million dollars to build the breathtakingly beautiful campus I have described in the beginning of this chapter. On three sides, it is bordered by the Aliso and Wood Canyons Regional Parks encompassing 4,000 acres of well-preserved wildlife. The new campus's principal buildings are named after world-peace activists: Mahatma Gandhi, Linus Pauling, and Ikeda Daisaku. From the beginning, this campus has been dedicated to world peace and harmony between humans and nature (Pulley), which is expressed through the construction of the "Peace Lake" and "Founders Hall," also described in the beginning of the chapter.

However, although the intent behind building a new campus was nothing but peace and preservation of harmony in all levels of human existence, a controversy occurred in 2003, which concerned SUA's affiliation with the Soka Gakkai International. One professor took legal action, alleging religious discrimination against faculty not affiliated with SGI. The administration refuted all allegations of sectarianism and religious discrimination, and the case was closed. But because of this unfortunate controversy, SUA no longer offers classes in Buddhism, and this distinguishes it from the other three Buddhist-based universities studied in this book.[11]

The Aliso Viejo campus was dedicated in 2007. Since then, it has become home for all SUA's graduate, undergraduate, and research programs. The Undergraduate College offers a Bachelor's degree in Liberal Arts with concentration in one or two of these areas: 1) environmental studies, 2) humanities, 3) social and behavioral sciences, and 4) international studies.

Methodology applied in teaching undergraduate programs is consistent with Mr. Makiguchi's principles that education must be delivered as a dialogue with, and personal empowerment of, an individual student, instead of relying on forceful feeding of information to crowds of students, who are then tested through a harsh system of examinations. One way in which Makiguchi's education is delivered is by ensuring reasonably small class sizes and small ratio between students and professors. The evidence that the small size class provides a critical condition for better learning abounds. Even the University of Phoenix recently posted on its site that the small size classes have five advantages which deeply affect the quality of learning, that is: 1) the course work can be easily adapted to fit the class, 2) no-shows are noticed and can be dealt with, 3) students receive significantly more feedback, 4) there is more opportunity to learn from peers, and 5) the transition to higher learning is easier to achieve (Jedeikin). Leonie Haimson, Executive Director of the "Class Size Matters," reports that the Institute of Educational Sciences (which is the research arm of the U.S. Department of Education) concluded that class size reduction is one of only four evidence-based reforms that have been proven to increase student achievement. Despite the undeniable evidence, the size of classes in regular colleges and universities grows exponentially, often for no other reason but the administration's demand for higher FTEs. By contrast, in all Buddhist-based universities studied for this book, the class size is kept small. This is understood to be necessary for practicing mindful learning—the hallmark of Buddhist education.

At SUA, all classrooms are kept small in order to allow close and effective time-space contact between students and professors. I was told that this was so important for this university's administration that, even as the campus was still under construction, president Habuki insisted that classrooms must be built in such a way that no reconstruction would ever allow them to hold more than 15 students. This is true even of classrooms for math, chemistry, and biology, although, on most campuses, these disciplines are usually taught in rooms sitting one to two hundred students, or more.

The interior design of SUA classrooms must be called ideal from a pedagogical point of view. There is natural light and access to fresh air in every room. An oval-shaped table is placed in the middle and students sit along the table's perimeter in chairs that are not only very comfortable, but allow them to change the direction of their attention with ease. The whole setting is so organized that the professor is constantly involved with students, staying in close proximity to all of them (and not just those few who sit in front rows), attentively observing the process of learning and noticing at once when a particular student struggles with a problem. It also makes it easier for the students to ask questions and give their responses while the learning process is ongoing, instead of doing this after the lecture, or during office hours, as it often happens when the classroom does not provide conditions conducive to professor-student interaction in the course of the classwork.

I must say that, as I investigated SUA, I developed a strong appreciation for its programs and style of education, largely because it emphasizes the importance of liberal arts and humanities. This university does so during a time when our national system of higher education is routinely slashing funds and reducing the breadth of courses in these very areas, at the same time, heavily supporting pre-professional and professional programs. It seems that SUA has purposely dedicated itself to teaching students how to appreciate their common humanness by placing special emphasis on, and providing generous financial and administrative support to, programs dealing with languages, music, arts, history, and literature.

To indicate the importance and interconnectedness of all these disciplines for the benefit of humanity and avoid competition between them, the administration decided to do away with separate departments, such as History, Modern Languages, Mathematics, Physics, Music, Theater, etc. Students graduate with a diploma which reflects successful training in all areas of liberal arts, while one or two specific areas must be focused on with an intention to continue personal and professional training in those areas for the sake of becoming a responsible global citizen.

Of specific interest is the "Learning Clusters" required for the BA program. According to the *2012–2013 Undergraduate Catalog*, "Learning Clusters" are research seminars designed to bridge theory and practice in the investigation of specific questions and bring about a specific product, educated outcome, or response needed to address a human problem. Students work in teams with one or two faculty. They propose, research, and model constructive approaches to local, regional, and global issues. Specific clusters are designed to help students learn how to apply a range of investigative and enlightened analytical tools in the discovery and presentation of the trends and ideas that bear upon the quality of the human condition (*Catalog*, 66–67).

One of SUA's graduates, Michelle Nunn, wrote in responding to my request, that she had participated in three learning clusters although only two were required. The three clusters she took were: "Poverty in Orange County," "Spiritual Health," and "Happiness." "The great thing about clusters," she wrote, "is that students get to work with the professor on creating the curriculum for the course. It is hands-on type of education. We went to various locations to do field-research. Working on a real-life project with a professor is definitely a powerful experience! One can study books for many years and still not understand the nature of the subject they study, or true demands of the profession one wishes to acquire. Learning clusters was definitely an awakening experience for me."

Another graduate, Eddie Ng, went to China, Yunnan province, to complete one of his Cluster Learning requirements. The goal of the course, according to him, was to study cultural differences between the ethnic minority groups in Yunnan and how the majority of the population was treating them. Students and faculty travelled to four different cities, interviewing government officials responsible for the equal rights opportunities for the Yunnan citizens. Then, they interviewed adults, teenagers, and children from ethnic communities to create a better understanding of the situation. Results of their findings have been submitted to the Nieves Family Foundation, which had awarded them the grant for this investigation.

According to the university's calendar, Learning Clusters occur in 3.5 week block periods in order to take full advantage of opportunities for field and service learning. Each year, several clusters, each including one or two instructors and seven to twelve students, travel inside and outside of the United States. Learning clusters are intended to: 1) develop habits of independent inquiry and study; 2) engender analytical and investigative skills and the ability to apply them to a specific problem or question; 3) enhance the ability to work collaboratively toward the completion of a common project; 4) foster a contributive ethic by working on issues that have a larger social significance; and 5) prepare students for their role as engaged global citizens and leaders.

Students can choose their cluster in one of two ways. They can work with a faculty advisor and then develop and submit a proposal to study a topic that interests seven or more students (however, there can be no more than twelve students in one cluster); or students may choose the topic of their cluster during registration by selecting it from the list of offerings already developed by the faculty.

Another advantage of the SUA undergraduate programs is a strong emphasis on studying the arts as a major way of transforming students into conscientious, contributive global citizens. This area of education, as previously mentioned, has been recently viewed as less essential than others. Already in high schools, as administrators attempt to maintain federal standards to receive government funding, they focus, almost exclusively, on math, writing, and reading comprehension. Not only are the arts viewed as less important for the successful life of our future generations, it is often admitted that the arts do not easily lend themselves to quantifiable measurement, and therefore, testing on them will not create benefits for the school (Progrebin).

College and university administrators, similarly, perceive development of students' artistic abilities as secondary in importance, or even as merely a recreational activity, for our entire higher education system is geared toward preparing the future workforce that, arguably, does not need skills in singing, painting, playing musical instruments, and comprehending and writing poetry, but requires proficiency in computer science, technology, engineering, and math. Artistic education, at present, is neglected nation-wide as tough economic conditions have set in and resources are strictly distributed. We often see art departments downsizing, or closing altogether. Recruitment for arts programs in average colleges and universities has become, virtually, non-existent.

Such a trend, however, directly contradicts scientific findings proving that education in the arts profoundly affects child and adult development. The effects are particularly crucial in the areas of our ability to concentrate on the task at hand, social-emotional stability and social-cultural identity, and the ability to further advance in cognition (Gardner, 44–53; Kindler, 290–96). This brings us back to the earlier discussed point of the "value-creating" education designed by Mr. Makiguchi. He repeatedly pointed out that it is supremely important to surround children, from their early years, with beauty, art, good manners, good taste, and elegance, so they can learn how to appreciate their own and others' humanness and creativity, and to become immersed in civilized and artistic ways of expressing themselves. It is not surprising, therefore, that despite the national trend requiring less and less art education, Soka University of America chooses a direction in the "value creating" pedagogy which insists that every student must be immersed in the arts, such as painting, pottery, calligraphy, creative writing, singing, dancing, and playing musical instruments. Browsing through the *2014–2015 Catalog* I discovered that the following classes can be taken to fulfill GE requirements for art education: Drawing, Sculpture, Creative Painting, Photography, Creative Dance, Piano Playing, Music Composition, Introduction to Songwriting, Music Composition with Computer, and Vocal Technique. Most of these classes can be taken at both introductory and advanced levels.

With this very goal—to stir students' creativity and immerse them in the harmony and beauty expressed through the arts—SUA built, in 2011, a magnificent and very expensive Performance Center. The university's theme-materials—cherry wood and travertine stone—were used in its building. Solar panels on the roof provide 15 percent of the energy needed to run the facility. Alaskan white cedar has been chosen for its finest acoustical properties on stage, and acoustics were designed by the famed Walt Disney Concert Hall acoustician, Yasuhisa Toyota. Local plants were installed in a rooftop garden which filters rainfall and provides oxygen. Its design has been executed to the highest environmental standards to teach students a lesson that arts and environmental wisdom can go hand in hand.

A few Soka professors who I have spoken to about this matter, expressed their firm belief that students deserve the best, rather than what can be afforded, when it comes to education in beauty and harmony, and that the money was rightly spent on building the Performance Center than on some other items. The Performance Center's administration, with the strong support from the university's faculty and students' parents, continues spending generously to invite specifically those artists who represent perfection in their chosen paths and at the same time passionately serve humanity with their gifts. Some of the artists who recently performed here include Yo-Yo Ma, Tokyo String Quartet, Julliard String Quartet, The Academy of the St. Martin in the Field, Chieftains, The Romeros, Jean-Yves Thibaudet, and Branford Marsalis.

The recent national trend of cutting support to teaching arts at American colleges and universities applies to the study of languages, as well. Administrative support for foreign languages programs is now in short supply due to financial struggles. But learning languages is viewed by Soka University of America as essential for becoming an intelligent and educated human being.

Its professors who are involved in "value-creating" education underscore the fact that it is through language comprehension that people understand each other. Thus, proficiency in English, and at least one foreign language, constitute requirements for all Soka graduates. A foreign language must be studied for at least two years; after that, students are required to travel abroad to the country whose language they have been studying. To ensure this condition can be easily met by all students, the cost of the foreign-language-based international study is included in the tuition.

Quoting from the *Catalog*, "the mission of the language and culture program is to foster the development of the linguistic proficiency and cultural awareness that are required in order for students to become well-educated global citizens. The underlying goals are to build communicative competence within a structured context; to strive for excellence through an eclectic, yet integrated variety of pedagogical methods, including innovative use of technology; and to instill a broad cultural awareness that will expand the disciplinary options open to students. A key task is to prepare students for the junior-year semester in another country . . . students are required to take a minimum of four foreign language courses one of which must be at the 202 level or above in the target language of the study abroad destination."

Learning outcomes for the Language Program state that, "Upon completion of the required courses students are expected to 1) have the linguistic proficiency to participate in the study abroad semester during their junior year, 2) have the cultural awareness to adapt to their study abroad environment, 3) further advance linguistic proficiency and cultural awareness in any of the languages offered at the University."

This description of language programs at SUA will be incomplete without discussing the "Bridge." "Bridge" is a program designed to help non-English speaking students fully adapt to the English-speaking environment and excel at other programs taught in English at SUA. It is taught in the summer before the beginning of a fall semester and, upon its completion, students take an exit exam. If the level of comprehension is lower than is necessary, students automatically remain in the program for a whole year, with the cost still covered by the initial payment of their annual tuition.

SUA also has graduate and research programs. The graduate school offers a Master of Arts degree in Second and Foreign Language Education concentrating on Teaching English as a Second Language.

The Pacific Basin Research Center at SUA conducts and supports research on the humane and peaceful development of the Asia-Pacific region (into which the Latin American border countries are also included). It awards grants and fellowships for research on public policy in the Pacific Rim, international security, and global social and education reform. The Center sponsors conferences, lecture-series, and graduate seminars (in which undergraduates are allowed to participate as listeners). SUA publishes *Annals of Scholarship* to promote the study of methodological issues in education with specific emphasis on interaction between arts and human sciences; and based on my conversations with its administration, there is a possibility of designing an MA degree in Soka Education.

STUDENTS AT SOKA UNIVERSITY OF AMERICA

About half of the student body is from the United States, with the other half coming from nearly 40 other countries and six continents. In 2012, SUA was ranked number one in the most international students enrolled among all colleges and universities by *U.S. News and World Report Best Colleges 2012.*

Unlike other Buddhist-inspired universities, SUA does not engage students in Buddhist studies, nor do they practice any form of meditation. All clubs and organizations on campus are cultural or athletic and entirely secular in nature. Some examples are clubs for Hawaiian and Polynesian dances, animal protection, Japanese Taiko drumming, Humanism-in-action, hip-hop dancing, scuba diving, and salsa dancing. Since 2002, students have been hosting an annual Halloween fair for the local community (including Aliso Viejo and the rest of the Orange County). They transform their recreation center into a "haunted house," provide food, game booths, face-painting, and other carnival-like activities for all who come to celebrate with them. On the first Saturday in May, students organize the International Festival, which involved 600 international performers and 9,500 attendees in 2012.

I interviewed several alumni in 2014. I asked one of them, Eddie Ng: "What do you value most about your education?" He answered, "The first course we take after entering SUA is "Core I—Enduring Questions of Humanity." This course refers to renowned philosophers such as Plato and Confucius. The purpose of it is to explore the profound and critical inquiries of those who sought beyond the superficial and pursued an understanding of our purpose as human beings. Taking this course before any other really sets the stage for our curriculum that always goes back to asking how we can use what we are learning in economics, fine arts, and environmental sciences in order to generate waves of peace in the world. I value the fact that my education taught me to find purpose in everything I do and use my skills to move humanity forward. I'm currently working in business which is notorious for causing discord in society, and yet, I learned to see beyond this bias because I was taught at SUA how to be rooted in reality in order to create a positive change."

I also asked Eddie how he was applying the knowledge and skills he received at the university to his postgraduate life. His answer underscored the cultural diversity of SUA where 40 percent of students have connections to 40 different countries. He said, "Outside the classroom, students interact and learn about different cultures by informally repeating phrases of multiple different languages from their friends. Although we study abroad only once, our international experience is supplemented by the close-knit friendships that we make on a daily basis. These experiences have helped me tremendously in my current job, where I am expected to interact with people from all over the world, ranging from our team in China to automotive parts suppliers in Eastern Europe. What others see as an intimidating endeavor is where my strength lies in the company. Currently, 100 percent of my projects require international communications. Cultural understanding and ability to see situation from a broader perspective and beyond what is superficial is what has allowed me to transition, in just five months of working at the company, from marketing intern to the project manager of an international cross-functional team."

NOTES

1. This is according to the SGI official site. Eight million followers are in Japan, while the rest are in North America, Europe, and other Asian countries.

2. Nichiren (1222–1282) is the founder of its own school of Buddhism (Nichiren shū). He disagreed with the Pure Land doctrines and practices taught by Hōnen. Hōnen taught that, by reciting the name of the Buddha Amitabha, people can be reborn in the Pure Land. Nichiren believed that the Lotus Sutra contained the Buddha's ultimate teachings and that people should place their faith in reciting the title of the sutra (practice known in Japan as "daimoku") which, by itself, is sufficient for liberation. In 1260, he wrote "Treatise on Establishing the Right [Teaching] for Securing Peace of Our Country" which was widely used by the Kamakura government in its attempts to avert political disaster. Throughout his life, Nichiren was arrested and persecuted many times for his teachings, but eventually, he was pardoned and died of natural causes on Mt. Minobu, leaving behind hundreds of written works. Nichiren Buddhism is a single-practice school, like Zen. It makes salvation accessible to all people willing to do the simple practice of chanting the title of the Lotus Sutra. Because he strongly believed that the End of the Dharma period of degradation had already arrived and people of Japan could be destroyed if they did not practice the "right kind" of Buddhism, he pursued an aggressive strategy of conversion and attacked other schools. This made him a controversial figure to this day (Mitchell, 301–306; Habito and Stone).

3. This organization is associated with the name of Tsunesaburo Makiguchi (1871–1944) who is considered its founder. Makiguchi's life and ideological principles upon which the Soka Gakkai was built will be detailed further in this chapter.

4. *SGI Quarterly* 72 (April 2013): 22.

5. *SGI Quarterly* 76 (April 2014): 24–25.

6. Ibid.

7. These two organizations have been discussed earlier in this chapter.

8. This work was published right before the outbreak of the Russian-Japanese War, when the danger was real that Japan might be colonized by Russia, like India and China were colonized by the European nations. The issues of education for the young generations were discussed in this work along with other serious issues pertaining to the contemporary state of humanity. He proposed how to develop global coexistence of all nations despite the widespread political, economical, and cultural competition (Miyata).

9. This translation appears on Soka Gakkai official website.

10. D. C. Holtom quotes from one of the politically minded educators of that era, saying, "The center of this phenomenal world is the Mikado's land. From this center we must expand this Great Spirit throughout the world . . . The expansion of Great Japan throughout the world and the elevation of the entire world into the land of the Gods (i.e., kami) is the urgent business of the present . . . " (Holtom, 107–8).

11. In the last few years, SUA has distanced itself from the Nichiren-based religious institutions in both Japan and United States. This, on one hand, has deprived the University of its powerful connections and privileges, but on another, it has completely cleared its good reputation. To understand the positive effects which connections to Nichiren's organizations provided, see Metraux, "The Soka Gakkai: Buddhism and Creation of a Harmonious and Peaceful Society." For a discussion of the more complex and controversial aspects of such an association, see Gamble and Watanabe, *A Public Betrayed: An Inside Look at Japanese Media Atrocities and Their Warnings to the West*. It is my personal opinion that SUA should resume teaching Buddhism in general, and Nichiren traditions, in particular. Hopefully, this will happen in the near future.

REFERENCES FOR CHAPTER FOUR

Bethel, Dayle. 1989. *Education for Creative Living: Ideas and Proposals of Tsunesaburo Makiguchi*. Ames, IA: Iowa State University Press.

De Melo, Silva. 2000. "Makiguchi Project in Action—Enhancing Education for Peace," *Journal of Oriental Studies* 10: 62-93.

Gamble, Adam, and Watanabe, Takesato. 2004. *A Public Betrayed: An Inside Look at Japanese Media Atrocities and Their Warnings to the West*. Washington, DC: Regnery Publishing.

Gardner, Howard. 1990. *Art Education and Human Development*. Los Angeles: Getty Publications.

Habito, Ruben, and Stone, Jacqueline. 1999. *Revisiting Nichiren*. Special Issue of *Japanese Journal of Religious Studies* 26, no. 304.

Haimson, Leonie. 2010. "The Benefits of Small Classes," www.classsizematters.org/benefits. Retrieved on June 25, 2014.

Heffron, John. 2009. "Soka Education as a Philosophy of Life: The SUA Experience," *Soka Education*, n. 2:143–48.

Holtom, D.C. 1922. *The Political Philosophy of Modern Shinto*, vol. XLIX, p. 2. Tokyo: Transactions of the Asiatic Society of Japan.

Ikeda, Daisaku. 1996. *A New Humanism*. New York: Weatherhill.

———. 2001. *Soka Education*. Santa Monica: Middleway Press.

Jedeikin, Jenny. 2013. "5 Benefits of a Small Class Size," www.phoenix.edu. Retrieved on June 26, 2014.

Kindler, Anna. 2003. "Commentary: Visual Culture, Visual Brain, and Art Education," *Studies in Art Education*, vol. 4, n. 3: 290–96.

Kisala, Robert. 2004. "Soka Gakkai: Searching for the Mainstream," in (eds.) Lewis, James and Petersen, Jesper. *Controversial New Religions*. Oxford: Oxford University Press.

Kumagai, Kazunori. 2000. "Value-Creating Pedagogy and Japanese Education in the Modern Era," *The Journal of Oriental Studies*, v. 10: 29–46.

Metraux, Daniel. 1996. "The Soka Gakkai: Buddhism and the Creation of a Harmonious and Peaceful Society," In Christopher Queen and Sally King (eds.), *Engaged Buddhism: Buddhist Liberation Movements in Asia* (New York: State University of New York Press).

Mitchell, Donald. 2013. *Buddhism: Introducing the Buddhist Experience*, 3rd Edition. New York: Oxford University Press.

Miyata, Koichi. 2000. *Ideas and Influence of Tsunesaburo Makiguchi: Special Issue of the Journal of Oriental Studies*, 10. Tokyo: The Institute of Oriental Philosophy.

Progrebin, Robin. 2007. "Book Tackles Old Debate: Role of Art in School." *The New York Times*, August 4.

Pulley, John. 2011. "Soka University Tries to Invent College," *The Chronicle of Higher Education* (January 2001): 18–19.

Sharma, Namrata. 1999. *Value Creators in Education: Japanese Educator Makiguchi and Mahatma Gandhi and Their Relevance for the Indian Education*. New Delhi: Regency Publications.

Soka University of America. 2012. *Undergraduate Catalog* 2012–2013.

Tsuji, Takehisa (trans.). 1979. Online collection of quotes from *Axioms of Tsunesaburo Makiguchi*, 1979 Japanese edition. http://www.tmakiguchi.org/quotes/.

Walker, Richard. 2013. "Soka University of America's 10th Anniversary," *SGI Quarterly* (April 2013): 1–3.

Chapter Five

Buddhist Pedagogy

What makes the educational experience at the Buddhist-inspired universities unique cannot be explained merely by their history and the professional degrees they provide. What makes them so different from hundreds of other universities across the United States is that education in professional fields and liberal arts is provided with the use of Buddhist pedagogy. This pedagogy has been tested by thousands of years of history in many different social and political environments. Now, it is being applied in twenty-first century America.

I had a conversation about Buddhist pedagogy with Prof. Richard Payne, Dean of the Institute of Buddhist Studies in Berkeley, California, and this is a paraphrase of what he said:

Since its affiliation with the Graduate Theological Union in the mid-1980s, the Institute has worked on formalizing expressions of the education philosophy that guides its instructional programs, and at the same time, can be applied to Buddhist-based education elsewhere. Four principles have been drawn from the worldview of this tradition which represent a careful balance with the values of Western culture:

1. Education is a process of mutual growth, so that ultimately, there is neither student nor teacher. Someone may at one moment be the teacher, but at another moment, will be the student. Faculty does not presume to reveal hidden wisdom to students; rather, they seek truth together. In this search, education is a mutual growth in wisdom and compassion.

2. Education is the exercise of mutual respect grounded in the teachings of the absence of any permanent self, or ego; and interconnectedness of all life is accepted as the main guiding principle. Mutual respect is the acknowledgment of the innate integrity of all sentient beings. Education flourishes only when student and teacher alike accept each other as they are and respect each other for what they aspire and strive to become.

3. Education, essentially, is a reformation of one's character, which advances only when change comes about in one's behavior and attitudes. True education is marked by those changes that increase one's practice of wisdom and compassion.

4. Education is a long process. It brings people from a state of suffering and frustration to an awakening from greed, hatred, and ignorance. Understanding gained at one stage in this process may not appear as actual behavior until a much later time. Thus, the success or failure of the educational process cannot be measured in terms of today or tomorrow. In contrast to the demands for an immediate payoff one finds frequently in present-day society and its institutions for higher education, value is given to humility and patience in the recognition that the benefits of education may not be immediately evident.

I agree with Prof. Payne that, in most general terms, Buddhist-based education must be characterized as an exercise in character-growth accompanied by mutual respect between students and teachers and that the true value of education, given and received, is not measured by the immediate payoff because education is understood as an investment in the future of humanity in terms of its potential for compassion and wisdom. All Buddhist universities I studied stand on this foundation and have designed a wide range of methods, approaches, practices, and exercises for teaching and learning wisdom and compassion, even as professional and liberal arts are being taught to students. For the mere sake of convenience, I am going to examine them in this chapter as classified according to:

1. Mindfulness,
2. Interconnectedness of all life, and
3. Right motivation for giving and receiving education. [1]

MINDFULNESS

In the last decade or so, mindfulness has become an important topic of investigation. It has been studied from multiple perspectives, including its proper Buddhist context and history; its applications for health, especially mindfulness-based stress reduction and mindfulness-based intervention; and its usefulness in completing daily tasks while coping with many challenges of our modern life (Austin; Batchelor; Chiesa and Seretti; Langer; Ly; Plank; Strum et al.; and Wayment et al.; and Wilson). "Mindfulness: Diverse Perspectives on Its Meaning, Origins, and Multiple Applications" by Williams and Kabat-Zinn covers most aspects of this term's definition and application, but for our study, the simplest definition will be most useful.

Described in the simplest way, mindfulness is an inner awareness of the things a person is doing in the moment she/he is doing them, and of the reasons for doing them. It involves being fully present, emotionally and intellectually, in what the person does and concentrating entirely on that. The state of mindfulness has been described in English by such terms as awareness, contemplation, being grounded, being present in the moment, and so forth.

As a professor, I teach regularly. I realize that mindfulness is absolutely required in the classroom, for it brings the most efficient results in teaching and learning, no matter what the subject area. I also realize that my students lack mindfulness to a greater extent than the students I taught ten years ago. When I look into the eyes of my students today, it is apparent that their minds have wandered. They have entirely forgotten they are in the middle of the lecture; they do not even remember they are sitting in the classroom. They think of the latest news a friend just texted to them, or about what they are going to do later that day, or what they are going to eat for lunch. Many students keep frantically texting, with their hands hidden in a pocket or under a desk, even after the lecture has begun. Some pretend to be typing notes from the lecture, but in actuality, search for something else, protected from my eyes by opened laptops. Today's students are so absent-minded that a simple question must be repeated several times until they comprehend what is required of them. Because their minds are so busy with things not pertaining to the subject of our study, even when a student finally grabs the core of my question, she or he cannot formulate an answer. During the last four years, I heard words, "I don't know," and "Please, ask me later," many more times than I would like to.

Against this background, I observed nearly ideal levels of mindfulness and comprehension in the classrooms of the Buddhist-based universities. I explain this entirely by the fact that practices of mindfulness are built into their teaching-learning methodologies. Mindfulness can be taught under different names and practiced through a variety of methods. What matters is that teaching and learning mindfulness becomes an important component of all programs. And this is exactly what is happening in the Buddhist-inspired education.

Naropa includes it in its "whole person education" which cultivates academic excellence through contemplative insight and infuses knowledge with wisdom. Dharma Realm Buddhist University teaches intellectual inquiry that proceeds, side-by-side, with the spiritual self-cultivation, so that the classroom is inspired by the contemplative life. A contemplative atmosphere surrounds all daily activities on its campus and promotes spiritual growth and inner enrichment.

University of the West is also guided by the principle of the "whole person" education which is informed by Buddhist wisdom and ethical values. Here, students, faculty, and administration work together to foster the ongoing dialogue between the Eastern and Western perspectives on learning; at the same time, classes in meditation are offered not only through its curriculum but also at the Hsi Lai Temple and in student dormitories. Soka University of America offers humanistic-values-based educational transformation which helps students become philosophers and world citizens; it employs methods for personal introspection and a socially active life as a way of learning and contemplating human suffering.

Mindfulness and contemplative modalities in learning are not unique to Buddhism. Judith Simmer-Brown, Distinguished Professor of Contemplative Education at Naropa University, suggests that by pursuing contemplative/mindful modalities in education, we return to the very roots of a liberal education in the West because these roots are grounded in the development of depth and wholeness that are synchronized with intellectual rigor (Simmer-Brown, 10). However, because most of our universities have adopted a market-model for all curricula and extra-curriculum activities and the practice of mindfulness has been assigned a rather low market value, it is no longer present in the classrooms. Students can learn most of the course-contents online and be graded online. Why would they value being mindful in the classroom? Even when professors make class-attendance a significant factor in grading they are helpless when it comes to turning attendance into mindfulness. In order to accomplish this, mindfulness must become one of the core values in our whole education.

So, it happens that on Buddhist campuses (unlike in the rest of our society), mindfulness, meditation, contemplation, introspection, and other forms of cultivated focused attention are viewed as being of high value. Because they are valued so highly, students take up this approach in their learning and to life itself. Since the fourth century, the time when the famous Nalanda University was created in India, Buddhism has been in the practice of merging meditation with all sorts of activities; this allows meditation and mindfulness to become a part of professional training in technology, sciences, and social leadership. Contemplative and meditative modalities easily become an integral part of a Buddhist-based curriculum, from liberal arts to business management, and from computer engineering to environmental sciences.

Students are involved in mindfulness in and outside the classroom, as well as in and outside the university itself. When practice of mindfulness is part of a course and part of a grade, course-descriptions and syllabi specify that this is the case. Students have a choice of the type of meditation/contemplation practices they pursue throughout courses with such requirements. At Naropa University, students choose from several wisdom-traditions—yoga, Jewish meditation, Taich'i, centering prayer, Aikido, Contemplative Brush-calligraphy, or Ikebana. The most widely taught form of mindfulness here is the Shamatha-vipashyana (it is prevalent in Tibetan forms of Buddhism), but Richard Brown, Professor of Contemplative Education, explains that the Shamatha meditation is taught not as a religious practice but as a "first-person" method for self-discovery and learning (Brown, 76–83).

Although meditation is not required in most of UWest programs, studying it is offered to all students, and the entire curriculum combines contemplative/reflective/meditative approaches to the subject with the "third-person" Western-scientific approaches. Moments of meditation and self-reflection are organically woven into lectures, discussions, and guidelines for preparing written and oral assignments. Additionally, UWest students themselves play a leading role in conducting meditation exercises before, during, and after classes. To illustrate this point, I provide here a digest of an article, "Second Overnight Sit Builds Diverse Sangha at UWest" by UWest student, Raymond MacDonald.

On Friday, March 30, 2012, all across Southern California, students were gearing up for a Friday night party. UWest students gathered for a very different kind of a party, the overnight meditation. The event was sponsored by UWest Contemplative Council, Office of Student Life, Chaplaincy Club, and BudaWest Club. The Exhibition Hall was transformed into a temple. Venerable Tenzin Kacho, an American Buddhist nun ordained by the fourteenth Dalai Lama, who served as a Chaplain in the U.S. Air Force Academy, gave a brief introduction to breathing meditation. Then, the room was reconfigured, and the four-fold assembly was created.[2] "What followed next," wrote Raymond "was nothing short of amazing. Through sharing different practices all night long, all present were united by a common intention to cultivate compassion and loving kindness toward each other and all of humanity. It became a rite of passage for the young students who have never participated in such events. Everybody breathed together, sat together, and walked together. When the morning came, a family-style breakfast and cleanup followed, and the temporary meditation space was restored back to the Exhibition Hall. It was clear that everyone present at the meditation has been deeply transformed" (R. McDonald).

During a Business Management class taught by Venerable Dr. Jue Ji, I listened to students' reports on how to develop mindfulness techniques, so that they can help with: 1) stress-release at a work-place, 2) sharpening co-workers' mental and psychological focus, and 3) providing mental and physical rest to people spending too much time in front of a computer. All participants, including myself, realized the extraordinary usefulness of learning how to take a brief, but powerful break from the computer, while grounding body and mind in the present moment. Staff members invited for participation seemed visibly relaxed and well-rested after these exercises. Students participated more actively during the second part of the lecture (after mindfulness exercises were done) than during the first.

At Naropa, each classroom building has a room (and some have more than one) whose exclusive purpose is the practice of meditation. Such rooms are simply decorated; they have cushions for traditional sitting, and chairs (or wooden benches) at the back of the room for those who have a problem sitting cross-legged. There is a shoe-stand to the side of the entrance, so that participants can remove their shoes before the practice. A sign posted on the door indicates that this is a meditation room and asks people to be quiet when walking around. Meditation can be practiced at any time and for any duration. When tired or in stress, faculty, students, and staff go inside a meditation room and restore their inner balance, bringing back their loving-kindness attitude toward people and the work they do. The UWest campus, likewise, has a room solely dedicated to meditation practices.[3] It is a very simple room with one Buddhist image placed by the central wall and wooden benches and meditation cushions on the other three walls. I spoke with the meditation instructor, a nun from Vietnam and graduate student at UWest. She told me that many students and faculty come during the designated hours to learn how to meditate. Levels of practice vary significantly among the monastics and students. Yet, beginners do not feel intimidated because the same guide-lines are given before a meditation session, no matter who participates. I talked to Chinese nuns, asking them if they feel "dragged down" because they meditate with students who have little or no practice. They explained that meditation is for the individual mind, therefore, it can reach a high state during meditation no matter what the environment.

After speaking to many of UWest's students, administrators, and faculty I realized that close to 90 percent of them engage in a regular practice of meditation and mindfulness. This helps them carry on with their daily activities, stay calm, and treat others with patience and compassion. "Mindfulness motivates for better performance in the classroom and in the office," I was told.

UWest has a unique connection with Hsi Lai Temple located only 15 minutes away from the university. At the temple, additional training in all forms of meditative and contemplative practices is available. Out of twenty students I spoke to, fifteen told to me they go regularly to the temple and participate in meditation activities there.

At the Dharma Realm Buddhist University, practices of mindfulness and meditation are mainly performed at the Temple of Ten Thousand Buddhas, located in the middle of the campus. Practice of meditation is required for specific tracks, such as Buddhist Study and Practice. The main temple can be reached by a few-minutes' walk from every other building on campus, and it serves as primary location for learning and practicing meditation. Many beautiful gardens for sitting and walking meditations are also spread around campus; one can practice in them any time. A regular three-week retreat is offered to all members of the DRBU community, including administration, students, and faculty. This event concludes each academic year in the early June period. During the semester, students willing to learn how to better meditate take the appropriate classes and conduct practices in the temple alongside the regularly meditating nuns and monks. Students at DRBU are fortunate to have the chance to ask the monastics, who are available on campus every day of the week, any kind of question they may have pertaining to their individual practice.

At Soka University of America, mindfulness is not taught through what we consider traditional Buddhist meditation. SUA is founded by the Soka Gakkai International which focuses on creation of human values, such as peace, happiness, and compassion toward all living beings. To accomplish this, SUA uses arts and mindful-social activities which guide students toward achieving these goals. What is practiced here may be better referred to as the awareness of human conditions aimed to alleviate human suffering. Students participate in on-campus activities that develop their sense of compassion toward all living beings, including plants and animals. They also sing and chant together, and chanting and singing in unison are scientifically proven to have a similar effect on the human brain as meditation (Horn).

INTERCONNECTEDNESS OF ALL LIFE

Equal in importance to mindfulness is the principle of "Interconnectedness of All Life." Like mindfulness, it is observed in every aspect of Buddhist-based education, inside and outside the classroom. Interconnectedness of All Life is referred to in different ways. In Sanskrit, it is "Pratitya-samutpada," or the "Simultaneous rising of all phenomena."[4] But it is also "Upeka," or "Equanimity observed in treating all life-forms." In English, such words as Interconnectedness, Interdependence, and Oneness are often used to express these ideas.

When "Pratityâ-samutpada," simultaneous rising of all phenomena, is clarified for the students, they understand that they are inter-dependent with other human beings and other life-forms for their very existence. The goal is to discard the illusion (enhanced by Western education) that we are separate and exist independently from each other. Central to this is the realization that an individual cannot be happy on her/his own, for even our own identity is a result of a network of connections and exchanges. Often, when this concept is taught in class, students are invited to see trees, sunshine, rain, and hard-working people (such as tree-loggers, truck-drivers, and machine-operators) in every piece of paper they use.

Thich Nhat Hahn provided the best exposition of this kind of philosophy in *The Heart of Understanding* (Thich), and Dr. Sid Brown wrote about this type of personal psychological transformation in her, seminal book, *Buddhist in the Classroom*. For her, Buddhist-based interconnectedness means that "everything exists in a matrix of all other things, so every thing affects other things, so nothing is somehow separate or exempt from anything else. Everything affects something else" (Brown 2008, 8). Seeing the world as interconnected changed the way in which Prof. Brown approached environmentalism—the topic she is teaching in college—and it deeply affected the way in which she saw life in general. To her, it became the only way to develop an appreciation of one's life

When the principle of interconnectedness is taught on the Buddhist-based campuses, teaching and learning do not stop after classes are dismissed. It continues in cafeterias and dining halls, for students eat together with their professors, and at the University of the West and Dharma Realm Buddhist University, monastics join students and professors as well. In this way, students are invited, once again, to think about every piece of food they put into their mouths and reflect on where the ingredients have come from. Without plants, soil, water, and sun, without all people working together to grow, deliver, and serve their food, they will have no food. In quite a similar way, and on many other occasions, students are guided toward the ultimate understanding that their personal successes cannot be accomplished without the successes of the whole community simply because we are all interconnected.

A significant component of this pedagogy is, first, intellectual grasping, and then, daily practice of the "Anatman," or "No-Ego." Anatman, as a philosophical term, points to the absence of a permanent self. "One's own self, as an entity that is disconnected and independent from all other entities, is an illusion," Prof. Guruge explains in his lectures. "It only appears that we are separate from everyone else and that our own selves have independent origination. This is definitely not so. Every thought I have is made out of the ingredients that have come from somewhere else. Every molecule in my body has, likewise, existed somewhere else before it became a part of my body."

Seeing one's self as a separate being needs to be corrected. It must be replaced by seeing oneself as the interconnected being which Thich Nhat Hahn calls the "We-being." It is my experience that people who work at the Buddhist-based universities see themselves as the "we-beings." From this position they understand their obligations toward work and students who came to study with them. From the president to the maintenance worker, from the dean to the professor, Buddhist-based education is interconnected; it excludes no one.

The difference in how students approach education on Buddhist campuses (compared to others) definitely rises from the sense of being interconnected. Students know that they really matter to everyone on campus. They know this is not just some game involving scores, GPAs, IDs, and dollars. They feel that everyone around them cares about them as real people, and this makes a huge difference in how they perceive their education and how they work toward it.

Unfortunately, today, this does not happen at many colleges and universities. Richard Arum and Josika Roksa describe in *Academically Adrift* a nationwide situation with undergraduate education which they call the "academic ratchet" (Arum and Roksa, 8–9).

While in high school, students hold the idea of college and university in high regard. They believe they will learn things which will not only make them professionals, but help them become better people, that is, help them understand what is morally right, help them appreciate the arts, sports, languages, and world history, and prepare them for more satisfying relationships with other people. But by the end of the first year in college, they realize that they are not treated like real people, that professors have no time to talk to them, and generally speaking, no one really cares whether they will become better people or not. They realize that, ultimately, it is all about numbers which are calculated in a business-like fashion. When students realize this, cynicism sets in, and they learn how to beat professors and administrators at their own game. If the numbers is all they want, students will give them numbers by using all means available, such as regular cheating on tests and exams, copying articles from websites, stealing other students' projects, re-cycling the same paper in several classes, and getting into legal battles with their professors over each and every point of their grade. Quoting from *Academically Adrift*, "[students develop] the art of college management, in which success is achieved primarily not through hard work but through con-trolling college by shaping schedules, taming professors, and limiting work-load" (Arum and Roksa, 4). In sum, in high school, they waited for the game of high school to be over, so that they can start a real life in college. Now, they begin to wait for the college-game to end, so they can start a real life somewhere else.

I am not idealistic about Buddhist-based universities to which I am dedi-cating this book and I understand that they have their own problems. But I know for sure that the "academic ratchet" I have just described does not apply to the Buddhist-based education, for, on Buddhist campuses, students are definitely treated like human beings. They are treated with full respect and dignity reaching far beyond what is required by the rules of political correctness. Buddhism-inspired professors and administrators, through their own study and practice of interconnectedness and meditation, know that, if they want to be respected by the students, they must respect them first. This applies to *all* students regardless of how they study or behave. By compari-son, at a regular college and university, a professor is not under an obligation to practice this form of respect. If she/he does not violate the university's moral code, this is deemed sufficient in terms of their accountability to students. But such accountability reaches farther according to the Buddhist-based pedagogy which operates on the notions of interconnectedness and equanimity.

In terms of equanimity, a classical example is found at Soka University of America. Its campus is unlike any other I visited during the several years of my study. It begins with the parking lot where one finds no signs which would designate parking reserved for people with special status. That is, try as hard as one may, one will not find parking A or B, or reserved for faculty vs. students vs. visitors. No parking is reserved for the president and provost either.

Social equanimity is observed in all offices and buildings on this campus, as well. Not only do administrators have no parking privileges, they are not given special buildings on campus either. John Pulley noted in "Soka U. Tries to Reinvent College" that the very absence of the administration build-ings expresses a deeply Buddhist philosophical position that the university's decision-makers must stay interconnected with other people and there should be no hiding places for them (Pulley).

Moreover, all SUA offices, from the deans' to the janitors', are the same size and equipped with furniture comparable in terms of price and comfort. With no ranks or other official distinctions, all members of the university are acknowledged as equal in their responsibilities to each other and to the students. This principle is so deeply embedded in SUA's pedagogy and social life on campus that even the president Daniel Habuki insists that everyone must call him Danny and never use his official title in addresses and conversations.

Respect for all life is vividly present on Buddhist campuses as it is displayed through the recognition that the environment is interconnected with, and thus affects human consciousness, and as a result—human academic performance. I will never forget the first impression I had of the classroom I visited at the Dharma Realm Buddhist University. It had large bright windows on three sides of the classroom, letting in fresh air and natural light. It had a simple, but outstandingly elegant piece of calligraphy on the far wall, and a flower-arrangement (just prepared by a professor) sitting on a low table by another wall. Students were holding cups of fragrant green tea as they quietly talked to each other and looked through lecture notes. Fifteen minutes were left before the beginning of the lecture.

I compared what I saw to the classrooms (on several different campuses) in which I have taught during more than twenty years of my career. Most of the classrooms I remember were filled with a sense of dread, boredom, and even foreboding. For the most part, they did not have any natural light or fresh air, and I could not detect any presence, whatsoever, of nature's beauty. These classrooms, definitely, did not sport any flower-arrangements or elegant paintings on the walls, although such things were always present in the administrative offices. So, I dare say that most classrooms in which professors (like me) teach today are characterized by dark curtains and artificial light, and by walls painted greyish-whitish, so as to avoid regular cleanups.

In juxtaposition to this situation, classrooms on Buddhist campuses are inviting. They are understood as being a part of the learning process because of the principle of interconnectedness. One just looks inside such a classroom and immediately wants to come in and be there. The sense of welcoming is not produced by luxurious furniture or expensive high-tech equipment. The happy vibe, so to speak, comes from the cleanliness and light of the environment, as well as from mindfully placed objects of beauty by people who teach and learn there and who truly care about the surroundings because they understand its effects on the human mind.

I have seen many beautiful flower and rock arrangements in Buddhist classrooms made by students and/or faculty wishing to express their connection to the world outside the classroom and to show appreciation of nature's generous beauty. In Buddhist classrooms, students are also given the privilege (and a responsibility) to organize their individual places of learning.

That is, students choose how and where to sit during the class-session. They can sit in regular chairs, on the floor, or on meditation cushions provided in the classroom or brought by the students. I interviewed a number of students at Naropa, asking them whether having a choice in the manner of sitting during the class makes any difference. They all enthusiastically answered in the positive. They explained that choosing the right, most appropriate position for sitting during class allows them to be more focused on the state of their mind and to better learn. Finding the exact configuration between physical body and consciousness maximizes the ability to learn and retain knowledge, for there is no longer a distraction caused by uncomfortable chairs and desks or by sitting too close to people or objects that can pull away your attention.

Furthermore, in a Buddhist-inspired classroom, a teacher does not usually stand or sit in front of rows of students whose desks are arranged in the formation of troops preparing for battle (i.e., perfectly lined horizontal lines forming rectangular or square geometric shapes). Instead, students and the professor sit in one big circle, indicating that they are connected to each other through the process of teaching and learning. But ultimately, what makes Buddhist-inspired classrooms so special is that students care about them. To them, these are not just some rooms they temporarily occupy, so that a market transaction of buying education at a very high price may happen. To them, these are places where they become mindful of themselves, of each other, and of the world around them; where the practice of interconnectedness happens each time they step in.

It is not surprising therefore, that environment-protection programs are the heart and center of all Buddhist-based universities' programs. Although protection of the environment is now taught at most colleges and universities because growing pollution threatens all of us, there is a significant difference between how teaching it is approached in Buddhist-based education and all others. In a nutshell, on most campuses the student learns about the environment in a classroom setting, but at a Buddhist university, the learning is practiced daily starting with her/his own campus.

Zigzagging in front of the Lincoln Building at the Naropa University, there runs the oldest irrigation ditch in Boulder known as Smith-Goss Ditch which was dug in 1859. Approximately a mile long, it watered fields at Boulder High School and the University of Colorado before it became a piece of NU property. At present, it is no longer functional, and there have been several proposals to eliminate the ditch and turn its one-mile long wild, green space into something "more useful." Yet, every time urbanization of the ditch was proposed, Naropa students vehemently opposed the idea of destroying this small piece of natural life on the edge of their campus. To them, this is not a useless space. To them, it is home to frogs and lizards and butterflies. They nicknamed it the Zen-ditch because a person can sit there, "at the end of all things," as they say it, and listen to the sounds of nature, feeling great tranquility in the heart.

Naropa students are also proud of, and give special protection to, sycamore trees which grow around campus, one of which is believed to be the tallest at 115 feet, and the oldest in Boulder. After the tenth student told me about the sycamores in just one day, I began to wonder—how many students on other campuses care about trees growing on their campuses? How many of them can even tell what kinds of tress grow there?

Protecting natural life daily through real environmental action is a hallmark of Buddhist-based environmental education. I was pleasantly surprised when I discovered on each of the Buddhist campuses that animal life is protected by students. Peacocks are protected by students of DRBU campus; squirrels by students at UWest; and groundhogs on the Paramita campus of NU in addition to the frogs and butterflies they care for on the Lincoln campus.

This brings me to a sad reflection on how green spaces (and the wild life with them) are being destroyed on my own campus. Just six years ago, I regularly saw jays, ducks, hawks, owls, and finches on and around campus, but not anymore. The habitat has been destroyed by what I must call the "greedy construction process," dictating that every piece of green grass must be turned into a building or parking space to justify its usefulness!

Understanding the usefulness of green spaces and a deep commitment to protecting natural life around us do not always happen naturally with our students. These things must be taught and practiced daily—then, and only then, young people will learn how to truly take care of our environment. I do not believe that by destroying beautiful oases of nature on and around campuses, we can teach students how to protect it. When there is such disconnect between what professors say during lecture and what people do to nature on universities' campuses, students cannot properly learn. This is the same as a parent trying to teach a child that telling a lie is bad, while lying to a spouse or neighbor at the same time. In Buddhist-based education, teachers know they must teach students by their own good examples. Every student present at the "Liberating Life" ceremonies regularly conducted by Master Xuan Hua was getting a message—animals are endowed with consciousness and they are sentient beings, like us. We have no moral right to mindlessly destroy them. One time, after Xuan Hua released pigeons stuck in the building, two of the birds did not fly away, but started following him everywhere. Instead of becoming frustrated or angry, he actually allowed pigeons to sit at his lecture. Those who had witnessed this episode tell us that Xuan Hua had repeatedly allowed birds to remain in the Buddhist Lecture Hall during his lectures and that he trained them to behave so as not to distract his human disciples (BTTS, vol. 2, 44–45).

Respect for all life and recognition of the importance of all life-forms are a constant theme in the Buddhist-inspired curricula. No matter what the subject, no matter who teaches it, this is one lesson all students will learn. It is present in business departments, writing and poetics programs, psychology, computer engineering, english, math, etc. By taking classes at a Buddhist-inspired university, students inevitably learn how to see the world from a position of the sanctity of all life, where every form of energy depends on all other forms of energy, and where short-term cultural, economic, and social gains are recognized as the inefficient use of natural and human resources.

Students are educated to treasure and wisely use their talents, as well. An outstanding example of this I found at the Naropa University. Near the cafeteria, there is a big bulletin board where students post announcements. Many of them read like this: "I would like to exchange a gift of picking up eatable mushrooms for a gift of knowing how to keep my room clean and organized (50 karmic points)." And, "I will exchange lessons in French (20 karmic points) for help with Biology." In 2010, during my visit to campus, I counted 50 announcements of this sort.

At Naropa, students are encouraged by their professors to avoid waste of any kind. So, students have designed a storage unit (open for everyone) where they store good things they no longer need. They bring desk-lamps, blankets, frying pans, forks, cups, etc., and place them on the shelves inside the storage room in a neat and orderly manner. People who have need of such things (students, faculty, staff, administration, and the local community) come and take them home. When they no longer need them, they return them, and the cycle continues. Everyone who has seen gigantic trash containers filled with students' possessions at the end of the semester will understand my strong sentiment of appreciating the wisdom of this simple solution to the problem. Actually—two problems. One is helping new students to get things they need after they settle on campus. (This is especially serious for those students who may not have extra money for buying necessities.) The second is the cost of cleaning dormitories after students have moved out.

Nowhere is the principle of interconnectedness as evident as in the teachings and practices of vegetarianism. In 2006, a report produced by the Food and Agriculture Organization of the United Nations pointed out that livestock production is a key source of carbon emissions, responsible for discharging 7.5 billion pounds of carbon dioxide into the atmosphere each year. That figure represents 18 percent of global green-house gas emissions. That revelation, as bad as it seems, was in fact a gross understatement, according to Robert Woodland and Jeff Anhang. In their article, "Livestock and Climate Change" published in 2009, they attributed 51 percent of global green-house gas emission, 32.6 billion pounds of carbon released into the atmosphere, to the raising of livestock and the production of meat, milk, and related products (Cheng Yen 2012).

I learned these facts during a lecture at the University of the West. I have never been presented with such data in lectures taught by other professors. Information omitted in the non-Buddhist overviews of those factors that contribute to green-house emissions also includes this: Fifty-five square feet of virgin forest must be cleared to plant a pasture large enough to produce a single pound of hamburger. In Latin America alone, 70 percent of forests have been reduced to pastures since 1970. To produce a pound of meat requires 21 pounds of grain (wheat and barley) or corn, and this is why livestock consumes a third of the total global grain production. In the United States, a heavily meat-eating country, animals raised for food consume 70 percent of the nation's grain output. On a global scale, hunger around the world could have been alleviated if the millions of tons of grain going to livestock were diverted to human consumption (Cheng Yen 60–63; UNEP 2010).

Buddhist universities teach the philosophy of vegetarianism and strongly encourage its practices (Epstein), even if it is only a few days a week, or as little as one meal a day. Not surprisingly, many students and professors at Naropa, UWest, and SUA are vegetarian, although they do not impose their views on others. At Dharma Realm Buddhist University, vegetarianism is strictly enforced, that is, no meat products are allowed, not only in its cafeteria but on its campus as a whole.[5]

The University of the West used to serve only vegetarian meals, but recently, out of compassion for those who cannot practice vegetarianism and suffer from the lack of meat in their diet, one dish of meat has been added to the vegetarian kitchen. Naropa and Soka universities are not strict in their vegetarian practices and allow meat consumption, because this is consistent with the practices of Tibetan and Nichiren forms of Buddhism upon which these two universities have been respectively founded. But at the same time, students are actively educated about the benefits of vegetarianism for health, environment, and spiritual progress (Kaza); at NU and SUA, several vegetarian options are always available in the cafeteria. Buddhist universities encourage the practice of mindful eating, and this definitely invites a reflection on the source of the meat, that is, the death of the animal. Thus, mindful eating becomes a reason for many students to switch to a completely vegetarian diet.

The principle of interconnectedness serves Buddhist-based universities particularly well when it comes to managing their financial resources. We know that American universities spend a good portion of their budgets on building, repairing and expanding parking spaces. Buddhist universities have devised a creative solution to the endless extension of parking around the university's parameters. At Naropa, students receive a bicycle and an annual bus-pass. At UWest, there are communally shared cars available for travel-ling between the Hsi Lai Temple and the university's campus, as well as for travelling between campus and various city locations. Communally shared cars are also used at NU, SUA, and DRBU.

Another way of saving money while practicing interconnectedness is to grow food on campus rather than to buy it from an outside supplier. At DRBU, gardens and orchards are tended to by all members of the univer-sity's community. The harvested produce is used in the dining hall and distributed to willing participants. Seventy percent of all food consumed at DRBU is grown in its vegetable patches and gardens. This saves the univer-sity nearly 15 percent of its overall budget.[6] At two universities, DRBU and UWest, students are involved in preparing ingredients for cooking and clean-ing dining halls and kitchens. This translates into yet another significant percent of budget savings. The practice of growing and preparing food, as well as cleaning after themselves, is transformational for the students. The food is good for their health because the ingredients are fresh.[7]

Buddhist campuses save on the cost of some work performed by the physical plant—cleaning of classrooms, offices, and dormitories, as well as taking care of and watering indoor and outdoor plants is often done by the university's community. In this way, money is saved and everyone learns real-life lessons in interconnectedness. "Littering in the classrooms and dor-mitories is practically absent because students take responsibility for their environment," the director of student life at DRBU told me.

Finally, the interconnectedness taught through the Buddhist education allows for a more positive outlook on life. Quoting from Soka University's article, "Interconnectedness," posted on its website: "If, as individuals we can embrace the view that 'because of that, this exists,' or in other words, because of that person, I can develop, then we never need to experience pointless conflicts in human relations. . . . On a deeper level, we are con-nected and related not just to those physically close to us, but to every living being. If we can realize this, feelings of loneliness and isolation, which cause so much suffering, begin to vanish, as we realize that we are a part of a dynamic, mutually interconnected whole."

RIGHT MOTIVATION FOR
GIVING AND RECEIVING EDUCATION

In his recent book, *What Money Can't Buy* (2012), Michael Sandel pointed out that we Americans have dangerously crossed over the moral limitations of markets. He specifically indicated that making our educational system "for sale" has become one of the more dangerous traits of America's most recent social transformation. He writes, ". . . some of the good things in life are corrupted or degraded if turned into commodities. . . . We have to decide how to value the goods in question—health, education, family life, nature, art, and civic duties." According to him, the danger of not doing so will result in that, "without quite realizing it, without ever deciding to do so, we drift from *having* a market economy to *being* a market society" (Sandel, 10–11).

One particular chapter of his book, "Paying kids for good grades," provides disturbing examples of how seriously our education has been already perverted by market-ideology. His examples include New York City paying fourth-graders $25 to score well on standardized tests, Washington, D.C., paying middle school students cash-rewards for attendance, good behavior, and turning in their homework (children can make up to $100 every two weeks), and Chicago schools offering their ninth graders cash for getting good grades—$50 for an A, $35 for a B, and $20 for a C (Sandel, 52–53).

A market-driven approach to education does not stop at schools. It permeates colleges and universities, as well. College and university students, to be precise, are not given money for doing well on their tests, but their financial support dwindles, or disappears entirely if they fall below the required GPA even by one tenth of a point. Corners are cut and new rules invented regularly to force students to graduate as soon as possible and not allow them to work on their education longer than is required for obtaining a degree. The degree itself is understood by most people working in the system of higher education, as nothing more than a license to obtain a job and make money, while the entire motivation for studying and graduation is based entirely on that concept. The result is that "increasingly, educators within the system have begun to raise their voices questioning whether organizational changes to colleges and universities in recent decades have undermined the core educational functions of these institutions" (Arum and Roksa, 1).

Because human nature is somehow wired to care about human values and not money alone, the promise of a good salary in the distant future just is not a strong enough motivation to graduate. Consequently, slightly more than 50 percent of American students who enter college leave with a BA degree (Selingo, ix). Because of that, the United States ranks twelve among developed nations in the attainment of higher-education by its young people. Research conducted from different angles of this problem (Astin 1993, Pope, and Arum and Roksa) indicates that the cost of education is not the main reason for the massive drop-out of students from national colleges and universities. More and more it appears the younger generations lack motivation for pursuing their degrees. A growing majority feel that they have been drifting through education and their life on campus without any purpose and without any result. By contrast, in Buddhist-based institutions, searching for, and finally realizing, the right motivation for education is strongly emphasized. Very much like mindfulness and respect for all life, finding the right motivation for education has been made into a foundational pedagogical principle observed on a daily basis in and outside the classroom.

The right motivation for education grows naturally from the eight-fold path, which is a basic system for moral training observed by Buddhist practitioners around the world. The eight-fold path includes: 1) right seeing, 2) right conceptualizing, 3) right speaking, 4) right acting, 5) right livelihood, 6) right motivation, 7) right mindfulness, and 8) right meditation.

There are many explanations of these eight phases of moral-psychological training.[8] I will provide here an explanation I usually give to my students which is based on a thorough study of the subject, the results of which have been simplified and adapted to modern day students' consciousness and vocabulary:

Right-seeing is seeing things and living beings as they are in that moment, that is, without forming quick unconscious judgments about their social value. For instance, when we see a homeless person, the right way of seeing her or him is to see a person and avoid rushing into judgments about this person's state of homelessness and its causes. The right way of seeing a physically attractive person is also to see her or him as a person and avoid rushing into mental judgments about specific elements of their attractiveness.

Right-conceptualizing (sometimes translated as "right-thinking") grows out of this deliberate lack of judgment in our seeing. It is enhanced through a proper mental process helping us realize more fully that a house (any house) is just a house, and we have freedom to create any form of judgment and/or attachment to it, or stay away from creating such judgments and attachments. In the same way, right-conceptualizing is applied to all material objects which have a potential (if improperly conceptualized) to cause us harm by generating in us greed, desires, sadness, jealousy, etc. Understanding and mentally examining every object and every living being without creating attachments, in essence, constitutes the right conceptualizing.

Right-speaking is the next step in the path of cultivation and is related to right-seeing and right-conceptualizing. As I explain to my students, if we believe that we see an attractive person, we speak to them differently than we speak to a person whom we believe to be non-attractive. We speak to a homeless person in a different way than we do to a friend whom we are about to ask for one hundred dollars. Right-speaking refers to the equanimity in our speech, meaning, we are to address every person in a kind and respectful manner without yielding to a desire to internally judge them based on their social value.

Right-acting follows the previous three steps. It is all about kind and compassionate treatment of all living beings. It is explained in Buddhist traditions that we must try to give our enemies and complete strangers the same respectful and kind treatment we give our friends. Right-acting involves simple daily actions such as walking down the street and trying not to harm anyone, opening doors for others, letting others take a better seat on a train, etc. It, ultimately, means acting with the awareness of others—one can open a door and slam it into the face of the next person simply because she/he is unaware of the next person, but the right action demands that we be aware of the next person and hold the door for them.

Right-livelihood means supporting one's material needs by doing work that is beneficial to all members of society and by consciously abstaining from work that can be harmful to others, no matter how generous the financial award might be. Examples of right-livelihood are: growing and selling organic food and other wholesome products, providing medical care and social service, teaching, creating material objects that are needed for healthy lifestyles, cleaning the environment, etc. Jobs that need to be avoided, if one practices right-livelihood, are: producing and selling alcohol and drugs, killing animals, engaging in sports which result in psychological attachments and physical injuries, entertainment that has a potential to seduce people to act immorally, etc.

Right-motivation primarily involves the constant practice of sustained awareness of the real motives behind one's decisions and actions. For example, when one offers to help a friend, the practice of right-motivation requires an examination of true psychological and mental motivations for this decision, namely: did she offer help because she wished to feel good about herself? Or did she offer help because she felt obligated and was afraid that, if she did not help, others would think poorly of her? Such false motivations for helping another person must be discarded and replaced by others which truly express our human interconnectedness.

Right-mindfulness is the practice of being mindful of each situation and finally making it a way of life. Right-mindfulness requires being aware of one's own state of mind and the obstacles one creates for practicing loving kindness towards others. It also requires the awareness of another's condition, especially if the other person is in a difficult psychological situation or experiences acute physical pain.

Right-meditation is the last phase in the eight-fold path, and it is also the one which connects the first and the last phases,[9] thus, creating a circle of practice rather than a hierarchy. What makes a meditation a right-meditation is not how well-practiced is one's posture and/or ability to remain calm during the entire duration of meditation, but rather, it is the intention, the reason why the person is practicing meditation in the first place. If one's intention is to become the most controlled and mentally strong, so that one can impose herself on others and win battles in mental struggles with them, this is not considered the right kind of meditation. The right-meditation starts with the right intention, which is to become a calmer person and less attached to material desires, greed, thirst for power, lust, etc., and then, be able to help others to do the same if they are willing to learn.

The eight-fold path in Buddhist universities is sometimes taught as a whole system and sometimes certain elements of it are taught in different subject areas. Eventually, all aspects of it are taught and internalized by students. Right-motivation for education is repeatedly underscored because it is understood by faculty and administration to be the foundation of success in both academic endeavor and the future life of a student. By visiting many universities, I observed that significant difference exists in the minds of students in Buddhist-based universities vs. those at other institutions. The difference is in personal attitudes towards learning and in the firm realization of the ultimate goals of education. When I asked students at non-Buddhist universities, "Why is it important for you to graduate on time and with a full degree?" many of them could not answer me. If I received answers, the typical answers were that they wanted to be able to support themselves financially, travel around the world by getting a job that involved travelling, or take care of their family, especially, if they were children of former immigrants without sufficient financial status. When I asked the same question at Buddhist-based universities, students (without exception) told me they want to become better people, protect the environment, create real communities, and help others; in sum, their reasons for studying well and graduating on time was to make *all* human life better, happier.

Students, administration, stuff, and faculty at Buddhist-based universities understand that helping other people requires compassion. In fact, compassion is all about understanding other people's suffering and finding the best way to minimize or alleviate it. This is why it is possible to say that compassion is the main motivation for giving and receiving education at Buddhist-based universities.

From my own experience teaching compassion to students, I know that it is the biggest life-changing surprise to them that they can be better motivated to work hard when feeling compassion for people who suffer and need their help, than by dreams of earning lots of money in a distant future. After many conversations and exercises (in and outside the classroom), students understand it completely. As one of them phrased it—"It is much more difficult to force yourself out of a comfortable bed at six in the morning for the sake of big money in ten years than by knowing that you can help others with knowledge and kindness you create though your education every day of your life!" After students "get it," they never go back to the exclusively money-and-career driven approach to their studies. Pre-pharm students stop "hating" chemistry because they realize that they do not learn it for a career and money, but because chemical formulas they prescribe will destroy or save people's lives. Students in engineering become excited about language requirements, instead of being grumpy about it, because they realize this is not just another hoop to jump through to receive social permission to make money, but sophisticated machinery they like to build must be built for real people with whom they must be able to properly communicate.

Being motivated by compassion for other people (and other living beings such as animals and plants) rather than by merely the prospect of a good job does not only make students work harder, but it brings real joy and satisfaction to their study and their whole life. People who practice compassion feel happier, their immune systems and health improve, their desire to study and to work increases, while their outlook on the future becomes increasingly more positive (Seppala et al.; Davidson). The Center for Compassion and Altruism Research and Education (CCARE) at Stanford University conducts research in many areas of teaching and practicing compassion. The Center's website and regularly updated blog contain dozens of articles which scientifically prove having compassionate thoughts and engaging in practices based on them affect development of the human brain in a positive way as no other type of activity can.

When we motivate our students by personal career and material gains only, we underestimate their humanity. We actually prove how poorly we understand our younger generation because the so-called "millennials" no longer see success in life in the same way previous generations have (Strauss and Howe). Material prosperity has been a crucial factor and powerful stimulus for personal and social progress in the decades after World War II, but younger people grew up surrounded by it, and therefore, it no longer has the same value and importance for them as it was for us. If we offer our students opportunities to create humanistic values, they will surprise us. Students I met in Buddhist-based universities surprised me because they all accepted a compassion-based perspective for their life's success.

Although it would seem impossible to teach compassion in a classroom (besides, from a perspective accepted in modern Western education, this is not even a responsibility of schools and colleges), from the position of Buddhist pedagogy, compassion needs to be taught at all levels. For, as the Dalai Lama pointed in his recent speech at the University of California, San Jose, "all technological accomplishments and social improvements will be lost because of an individual's lack of moral values, specifically, lack of compassion for his fellow human beings."

Kathleen McDonald summarized methods for teaching compassion in *Awakening the Kind Heart: How to Meditate on Compassion*. The methodology she describes can be taught at all levels and in all types of education. A set of simple, regularly practiced exercises which awaken empathy for others and beget a more compassionate view of humanity starts with developing compassion toward one's own existence. Compassion toward oneself is different from pitying oneself (Mackenzie). It is based on understanding that human nature is imperfect and prone to suffering, but also capable of minimizing suffering by letting go of attachments, judgments, and expectations.

Having compassion toward oneself, first of all, involves treating one's physical body in a respectful way by giving it healthy food, plenty of rest and exercise, and also by nurturing one's emotions through wholesome friendships and harmonious family relationships.[10] Once this attitude is established, caring for human wellbeing is extended to the nearest groups of people, such as a circle of friends and the family; eventually, it is extended to all humanity (Batchelor, 25–27, 62–65; McDonald, 19–117).

There are specific forms of meditation, typologically called the Metta-meditation,[11] about which I learned from the Buddhist-inspired faculty. Some are described and explained by Miller and M. Batchelor (Miller, 61–63; M. Batchelor). Students are first guided to become calm in their mind through breathing, then, asked to remember feelings of loving kindness they experienced in the past as a result of someone doing something nice for them, or as a result of their doing something nice for another person. Then, they are guided to develop and hold the sense of loving kindness toward other people. Based on interviews with students who practiced this, experiencing loving kindness toward others (instead of feeling frustration, annoyance, and competition) makes them feel very happy and more inspired toward their academic work. Higher levels of the Metta-meditation include holding feelings of compassion for prolonged periods of time, eventually throughout a full day of activities. It is also considered to be an advanced form of this meditation if one can hold thoughts and feelings of loving kindness toward one's personal enemy, people who had harmed one's family, or people considered to be the worst by contemporary social judgment, such as people in prisons.

After the Metta-meditation is practiced in class, the next step is to ask students to conduct simple actions of kindness outside the class while holding this sense of compassion toward others. Actions include holding a door for another person, greeting a visitor who is new to campus, asking friends if they need help with something, or assisting an elder person in crossing a busy and potentially dangerous intersection. Many of my students did these exercises as a part of their homework in a class on Buddhist traditions I teach at my university. All of them reported to me (in their writing assignment) that they have felt so good, so happy during the entire time they kept this state of compassion toward other people. A smaller percent of my students attempted compassionate behavior toward people they considered enemies. Here, too, students reported good results, such as cessation of animosity toward an emotionally cold father, or restoring a normal relationship with a rebellious younger sister.

Developing loving kindness toward all living beings and serving them with compassion in all situations, especially in a chosen professional capacity, must be considered the most important motivation for students, faculty, staff, and administration at Buddhist universities. But there are, of course, other and closely related motivations, as well. One of them I will briefly discuss: motivation to create a better human community.

Benefiting communities, both local and global, is often mentioned as an important educational goal on American campuses. The difference between how this subject is approached in non-Buddhist classes and those that are Buddhist-inspired is in the presence of hypocrisy in the former and the lack of it in the latter. It is similar to how environmental protection is taught in Western education—during the lecture, students are told they must protect the environment, but the moment they walk out of the classroom, they see trees being cut down and birds chased away for the sake of a new parking space on campus. Because hypocrisy has never been good for teaching behavior we want people to learn, in Buddhist classrooms, building a better community is not postponed for another time and place. Community, referred to in Buddhist traditions as Sangha, is built every time students come to class.

Sid Brown described in length the process of building Sangha in the classroom (Brown, 31–50). In "Viewing Each Other with Kindly Eyes: Community in the Classroom," she writes, "I emphasize the integrity of our community when I recognize repeated absences of a student as losses to all of us, not just to the missing student. If I know a student is sick, I invite members of the class to check on her and ask if they can help. During one semester, when a student's sibling died and he left to be with his family, I brought a card to class and each of his classmates and I signed the card for him. That student's loss was our loss—out of compassion and honesty, we recognized that in a community action: the signing of a card" (Brown, 33–34).

Another specialist in Buddhist education, John Miller, writes: "Holistic education seeks to develop community within classrooms . . . and also connects students to the community that surrounds the schools . . . the teacher attempts to create an atmosphere of trust that supports the development of community. This is done through conveying respect for students, listening attentively, and being genuine in conveying one's feelings. Mindfulness . . . is one of the principal means of doing this" (Miller, 105–6).

I saw many times how community was built in Buddhist-inspired classes, and I learned, to a limited degree, how to do it in my classes. A few principles I find to be most fundamental to the process. They are:

1. *Emotional honesty.* If I feel upset by the lack of students' enthusiasm in completing assignments, I do not hide my emotions, but I do not randomly display them either. The whole class does a five-minute meditation, and then I ask my students' permission to honestly share my feelings about their failure on the assignment. They understand me very well because I am honest, but not angry, and provide no judg-

ment. I simply share with them how it makes me feel as their teacher. I ask them not to feel guilty, but instead, be honest with themselves and understand why they have not completed the assignment. I sit with them in a big circle and ask a random student to start explaining reasons for not completing an assignment. After that, I give students 15–20 minutes to finish and revise the reading. This is usually followed by one of the best discussions I have in class. I always admit to my mistakes and apologize to students, and they do the same to me. In this way, mutual respect is established and the sense of being a community (rather than random gathering of individuals) always helps us to do our work.

2. *Connecting to my students' humanness.* Students are more than their social function in the institution of higher learning. They are people. They are humans, individuals, with their own personalities, emotions, worries, and needs, and they want and must be recognized as human beings, not just students. During our first meeting, I ask students in my class to introduce themselves by giving us the name they want me and other students to call them, by telling us about their favorite things in life, and by describing what has attracted them to the majors and minors they pursue. At the end of the first meeting, I ask them to send me a file containing their favorite self-image and the things shared in class. These files are for my private use only and will never be shared with anyone else. I spend two weeks at the beginning of each semester remembering my students' names and faces and what they love to do and what they want to study as their future professions. When I teach, I address their humanness, not only their studentship.

3. *Making connections between what is taught and what has been learned.* At some point in my lecture, I ask students to close their eyes, go deep into their mind, and recollect everything they have learned from the beginning of the lecture to the present moment. I give five to seven minutes to this exercise; then, I gently ring the bell and they open their eyes. Every student shares what he/she has learned. After this, I ask them to think of real-life situations in which they will be able to use what they have learned. And we make a practice of it. For two to three weeks, they consciously apply to real life what they have learned in class, and then write a report to summarize the practice.

At Buddhist universities, community built in the classroom is extended to other people in a local and global sense. I explained in chapter four that Soka University of America has cluster-learning requirements during which students meet real people and try to solve their real problems. Naropa has a similar requirement called service learning trips. University of the West provides regular opportunities for service through its connection to the temple and temple-affiliated charity organizations. The degree to which community-oriented learning is not only valued but actually required in Buddhist-based education is remarkable and usually not found in other types of institutions.

A community-based approach has its foundation in the philosophy of no-self and no-ego, described in the "Interconnectedness" subchapter of this chapter. Unlike the Western view of selfhood, Buddhists underscore that nothing can exist without the other. This philosophical position underpins the community-based principle of education. In Western paradigm, students are told they must learn, so they can provide for themselves, become well-positioned in society, and then (when they have enough for themselves and their families), engage in charitable activity. From a Buddhist perspective, one's wellbeing can never be accomplished if one does not realize that one's wellbeing is connected to that of the rest of the society.

NOTES

1. Buddhologists must be aware that certain explanations of Buddhist terms and categories, provided in this chapter, may appear simplistic. Such simplicity has been pursued on purpose because potential readers of this book include not only Buddhologists but specialists in higher education whose knowledge on the subjects of Buddhist is limited.

2. Four-fold assembly includes 1) female monastics, 2) female lay practitioners, 3) male monastics, and 4) male lay practitioners.

3. It also has a Meditation Pavilion overseeing the mountains which I described in the beginning of chapter one.

4. In Pali, the same term is known as "Pattica-samuppada." This term is also translated as dependent co-rising, dependent origination, and mutual causality (Macy, xi–xii).

5. This can be compared to prohibiting alcohol consumption on most campuses. Persons caught with alcohol will be reprimanded, and this will be reflected in their personal record. If the offense is repeated, student or faculty can be expelled. The same degree of strictness applies here to the consumption of meat.

6. This is according to my interviews with DRBU administration; this information also appears on the university's website.

7. The influence of the idea of being mindful of what we eat and of where the ingredients have come from recently spread to non-Buddhist campuses; nation-wide, students started growing their own food, including at the Pomona, Luther, Fort Lewis, Boston, Knox, Edmonds, and Wilmington colleges, and two UCs in Davis and San Diego.

8. For a historical approach, see McDonald, 53–61; for a comparative ethics approach, see Chang.

9. This means that, in order to start seeing people and objects without rushing into unconscious judgment about them ("right-seeing"), one must practice the initial-phase meditation.

10. Learning how to treat oneself with compassion, really, is the first step, for as I explain to my students: "You cannot give to others what you do not have. If you don't learn how to care for yourself, you will not be able to care for others."

11. Metta is usually translated as "loving kindness."

REFERENCES FOR CHAPTER FIVE

Mindfulness

Austin, James. 2000. *Zen and the Brain; Toward an Understanding of Meditation and Consciousness*. Cambridge, MA: The MIT Press.
Batchelor, Martine. 2011. "Meditation and Mindfulness," *Contemporary Buddhism* 12, 1: 157–64.
Brown, Richard. 2011. "The Mindful Teacher as the Foundation of Contemplative Pedagogy," in J. Simmer-Brown (ed.), *Meditation and the Classroom*. New York: State University of New York Press.
Chiesa, A., and A. Seretti. 2009. "Mindfulness-Based Stress Reduction for Stress Management in Healthy People: Review and Meta-analysis," *Journal of Alternative and Complementary Medicine* 15.5: 593–600.
Horn, Stacy. 2014. *Imperfect Harmony: Finding Happiness Singing with Others*. New York: Workman Publishing.
Langer, Ellen. 1997. *The Power of Mindful Learning*. Cambridge, MA: Perseus Books.
Ly, Boreth. 2012. "Buddhist Walking Meditations," *Positions* 20. 1: 267–85.
Mackenzie, Matthew. 2008. "Self-Awareness without a Self," *Asian Philosophy* vol. 18: 245–66.
Plank, Katarina. 2010. "Mindful Medicine: The Growing Trend of Mindfulness-based Therapies in the Swedish Health Care System," *Finnish Journal of Ethnicity and Migration* vol. 5: 47–55.
Strauss, William, and Neil Howe. 2000. *Millennials Rising: The Next Great Generation*. New York: Vintage Original.
Strum, Deborah, et al. 2012. "The Elements: A Model of Mindful Supervision," *Journal of Creativity in Mental Health* 7.3: 222–32.
Wayment, Heidi, et al. 2011. "Doing and Being: Mindfulness, Health, and Quiet Ego Characteristics among Buddhist Practitioners," *Journal of Happiness Studies* 12.4: 575–89.
Williams, J. and J. Kabat-Zinn. 2011. "Mindfulness: Diverse Perspectives on Its Meaning, Origins, and Multiple Applications at the Intersection of Science and Dharma," *Contemporary Buddhism: An Interdisciplinary Journal* 12.1: 1–18.
Wilson, Jeff. 2014. *Mindful America: The Mutual Transformations of Buddhist Meditation and American Culture*. New York: Oxford University Press.

Interconnectedness

Brown, Sid. 2008. *A Buddhist in the Classroom*. New York: State University of New York Press.
Cheng Yen. 2012. "Vegetarianism," *Tzu Chi*, winter 2012: 60–72.
Epstein, Ronald. 2006. "Buddhist Resources on Vegetarianism and Animal Welfare," www.sfsu.edu.
Goodland, Robert, and Jeff Anhang. 2009. "Livestock and Climate Change," *World Watch*, November–December 2009.
Kaza, Stephanie. 2005. "Western Buddhist Motivations for Vegetarianism," *Worldviews: Global Religions, Culture and Ecology* 9.3: 385–411.
Macy, Joanna. 1991. *Mutual Causality in Buddhism and General Systems Theory: The Dharma of Natural Systems*. Albany, NY: State University of New York Press.
UNEP (United Nations Environmental Program). 2010. *Assessing the Environmental Impacts of Consumption and Production*.
Woodland, Robert, and Anhang, Jeff. 2009. "Livestock and Climate Change." *World Watch Magazine*, Vol. 22, No. 6. Nov/Dec.

Right motivation

Arum, Richard, and Josipa Roksa. 2011. *Academically Adrift: Limited Learning on College Campuses*. Chicago: University of Chicago Press.

Astin, Alexander. 1993. *What Matters in College? Four Critical Years Revisited*. San Francisco: Jossey-Bass Publishers.

Batchelor, Steven. 1998. *Buddhism without Beliefs*. New York: Riverhead Books.

Bond, George. 2004. *Buddhism at Work; Community Development, Social Empowerment, and the Sarvodaya Movement*. Bloomfield, CT: Kumarian.

Brandon, David. 1976. *Zen in the Art of Helping*. Boston: Routledge.

Chang, Otto. 2012. "Accounting Ethics Education: Comparison with Buddhist Ethics Education Framework," *Journal of Religion and Business Ethics* 3: 1–22.

Davidson, Richard, 2002. "Toward a Biology of Positive Affect and Compassion." In (ed.) Davidson, R. and Harrington, A. *Visions of Compassion: Western Scientists and Tibetan Buddhists Examine Human Nature*. New York: Oxford University Press: 107–31.

Davidson, Richard, and Anne Harrington. 2002. *Visions of Compassion: Western Scientists and Tibetan Buddhists Examine Human Nature*. New York: Oxford University Press.

McDonald, Kathleen. 2010. *Awakening the Kind Heart: How to Meditate on Compassion*. Boston: Wisdom Publications.

Miller, John. 2006. *Educating for Wisdom and Compassion*. Thousand Oaks, CA: Corwin Press.

Pope, Loren. 2012. *Colleges that Change Lives*. New York: Penguin Books.

Salzberg, Sharon. 1997. *Loving Kindness: The Revolutionary Art of Happiness*. Boston: Shambala Publications.

Sandel, Michael. 2012. *What Money Can't Buy: The Moral Limits of Markets*. New York: Farrar, Straus and Giroux.

Selingo, Jeffrey. 2013. *College (Un)bound: The Future of Higher Education and What it Means for Students*. Boston: New Harvest.

Seppala, E., et al. 2013. "Social Connection and Compassion: Important Predictors of Health and Well-being," *Social Research* 80.3: 411–30.

Simmer-Brown, Judith, and Fran Grace. 2011. *Meditation and the Classroom: Contemplative Pedagogy for Religious Studies*. New York: State University of New York Press.

Thich, Nhat Hahn. 1978. *The Heart of Understanding: Commentaries on the Prajnaparamita Heart Sutra*. Berkeley, CA: Parallax Press.

Wallace, Alan. 2004. *The Four Immeasurables: Cultivating a Boundless Heart*. Ithaca, NY: Snow Lion Publications.

Conclusion

Conversation

I would like to conclude by inviting a conversation about what can be learned from Buddhist-based education examined in this book, so that, hopefully, useful changes can be created in the quality of our higher education—changes which will inspire younger generations to truly value and enjoy the process and take new pride in graduating. The first change, which can be easily created on campuses and which will cost us no money, but will bring about a significant difference in how educators and students approach academic studies is a campus-wide introduction of meditation practices.

Our lives are so fast, and information we receive every day is overwhelming. Students across the country are overwhelmed not only by the amount of academic work assigned to them, but also by their lives' increasing challenges. Meditation is proven to help students achieve calmness of mind and to develop a positive attitude towards life. Meditation helps students to learn better and to better retain what has been learned. Scientific proof of the positive effects of meditation on people of all ages, but especially on younger generations, abounds. *Zen and Brain* (Austin), is a collection of one hundred and fifty-eight pieces of research on improvement of brain function acquired through the practice of Zen. Along with studies already mentioned in this book (S. Brown, Simmer-Brown 2011, S. Batchelor, M. Batchelor, Miller, Ly, Wayment, and McDonald),[1] it is yet another convincing argument in favor of teaching meditation in the classroom.

A number of universities that are not Buddhist-based, such as Stanford, Cambridge, and Brown, have already recognized the fact that meditative practices are of high value when it comes to improving students' and faculty's performance; consequently, they established centers for promoting med-

itation on their campuses. Voices in favor of more mindful, meditative approaches to education come from many directions, not necessarily Buddhist.
One example is *The Power of Mindful Learning* by Ellen Langer who under-
scores the problem with teaching skills to students until they learn them as
"second nature," i.e., without self-reflection and mindfulness. Such methodology, according to her, removes the awareness of why things need to be
learned in the first place. In such "mindless" education, awareness of the true
goals of learning, namely, personal development and creating better communities, disappear, along with a healthy desire for learning, for knowing, and
for understanding (Langer, 10–11). She states, "Learning the basics in a rote,
unthinking manner . . . ensures mediocrity . . . it deprives learners of max-
imizing their own potential for more effective performance and [takes away]
enjoyment of the activity" (Langer, 14–15).

Although it may seem difficult to introduce meditation to campus and
academic life, it actually isn't. University of the Pacific where I teach can be
used as an example. I am supported by the administration to teach meditation
in all of my classes. Over the years, I have collected a large portfolio of
students' responses to the usefulness of meditation in the improvement of
their academic and personal lives. One student wrote: "I enjoy it when we do
meditation in the classroom. It is relaxing and it takes away stress. When we
meditate, I stop worrying about my daily schedule and clear my mind. After
that, I can concentrate better in the class that Prof. Storch teaches, and in all
other classes, as well. . . . I also realize that, when I meditate regularly, my
life becomes a lot calmer and I experience no stress . . . it is quite a shame
that all students are not taught how to meditate." Another student admitted,
"When I meditate, I always feel a sense of light and ease in the upper part of
my chest. I believe this happens because I am a very emotional person, so my
heart always feels heavy because I care so much about other people. But
when I meditate, I am able to release my emotional stress. I feel peace. I
decided to meditate regularly on my own because I do not want to stress
myself and pass stress onto my friends. Meditation is especially helpful
during examination periods."

Meditation at Pacific is taught to the athletes by sport science faculty who
understand the benefits of meditation in sport training and performance
(Jackson). Relaxation through meditation is offered between classes by Well-
ness Center staff, and according to students' reports, it helps them to remain
calm and to mindfully deal with their personal and academic problems. Meditative and contemplative practices (Qigong, Yoga, and Reiki, in addition to
sitting and walking meditations) are offered through weekend classes at the
Center for Professional and Continuous Education, as well as through Pacific
Seminar—a course required for all students, where they learn about "Good
Society."

In my experience, in order to teach meditation across curriculum, no outside funds or extra-pay is required—only our understanding of how important it is for creating positive changes in our students' lives, and for their personal and academic success. Our universities have succeeded in rooting out ethnic, racial, cultural, and sexual prejudices. It happened as a result of constant university-wide efforts. The same model can be used for disseminating practices of meditation and mindfulness.

Another change which must be made if we seriously care about our younger generation is the return of ethical and spiritual dimensions into higher education. George Marsden embarked on a long journey in *The Soul of the American University*, examining the history of our universities from the era he characterized as "Protestant Establishment" to the modern phase which he characterized as the "Established Non-belief." In the end, he came to the conclusion that, in order to uphold American democratic principles in education, such as freedom of thought, intellectual inquiry, and ideological pluralism, it was not necessary to have chased away each and every form of spiritual, ethical, and religious engagement in the classroom and curriculum (Marsden, 429–40). Yet, this is exactly what has happened. According to M. Edwards, questions of spirituality became one of the lowest priorities on our campuses. According to the statistics in his book, 62 percent of students at forty-six different universities reported that their professors never provide an opportunity to students to discuss spiritual, ethical, or religious matters in class, including questions pertaining to the meaning of life.

But Loren Pope in *Colleges That Change Lives* writes that colleges which change people's lives do so precisely because they offer education from the position of a student's life-path and spiritual-ethical quest for the meaning of it all. She writes that such colleges focus on a student as a human being and that teaching is an act of love, with students and faculty working closely together and younger and older generations listening to each other, while the true goals for education are regularly discussed and not hidden behind the business-like jargon (Pope, 1–5).

Parker Palmer, author of *To Know as We Are Known: Education as Spiritual Journey* provides a good summary of his life-long investigation into why it is so crucial to have an ethical and relationship-built dimension in education by saying: "The crucial difference between observing and relating is that a relationship is always two-way. As we use the full range of human instruments to know reality, we find that we are also known. The world we can know through our senses and our logic is a world that cannot speak back to us, speak to us about ourselves. With this limited mode of knowing, not only does the non-human world remain inarticulate, but the human world is deprived of *its* voice as we transform people into objects, things. But when we know through our other capacities as well—empathy, intuition, compassion, faith—we pick up the world's subtle signals, its subvocal speech, its messages to us about our limitations and responsibilities and potentials. When we allow the whole self to know in relationship, we come into a community of mutual knowing in which we will be transformed even as we transform" (Palmer, 54).

As the result of several years of research in the success of Buddhist-based universities, I am convinced that it is not the Buddhist foundation per se that makes it into such a positive pedagogical experience (woefully absent on many other campuses), but a foundation in ethical relationships between all parties involved. It is the mutually loving, compassionate, and respectful ways in which members of the university's community treat each other while remaining fully professional in their respective fields. Equally important is a strongly held conviction that success in education cannot be measured by how quickly graduates obtain jobs, nor by how large salaries are in the first year of employment. Harvard University President, T. Faust, recently interviewed by NPR, explained that she is opposed to the newest form of government assessment that measures educational success by graduates' salaries in the first year of employment. Very much like Buddhist educators at UWest, DRBU, Naropa, and SUA, she underscored the fact that education is different from other forms of social service because its results cannot always be known instantaneously; this is because education is a life-long journey and the results of good teaching may not be apparent until several years later, when a student matures and begins to thrive due to the professional and ethical training received at a university.

According to Buddhist-inspired faculty, teaching is like starting a garden—one must wait for years to truly see the results; and sometimes, results exceed all expectations, and sometimes, they can be disappointing. Nevertheless, unless education is understood as a process leading to personal transformation and ethical growth which will bring about a greater sense of responsibility to the entire human community and joy in serving other living beings, one does not speak of education, merely training in professional skills.

We must remind ourselves why a liberal arts education has become the primary form of education in Western civilization. Liberal arts represents knowledge which only free citizens of Greek poleis were allowed to pursue. This was an education steeped in the concerns of human wellbeing, searching for the meaning of life and nature of the whole world. An altogether different form of education was imposed on slaves. They had to learn how to build walls, grow grapes, and make pots without ever receiving time and opportunity to ponder why they were doing all these things in the first place.

In my humble opinion, what harms our higher education the most is not the financial situation, but social hypocrisy. We teach students not to lie while we lie to them all the time. We teach them to protect the environment while we destroy trees and birds on campuses for the sake of new buildings which generate more funds. We teach them to be honest, but we do not hold ourselves to the same moral standards which we apply to them. What we do not realize is that we will grow old in the world created by our former students. Because teachers (whether they acknowledge this or not) have this power to impact the future of humanity, a teacher has always been one of the most respected positions in society. We must remember that, although other professions, say, food-preparers, street-cleaners, and auto-makers are highly respectable, too, poorly prepared food can be sent back to the kitchen, unclean streets can be made cleaner, and bad cars can be reclaimed by hundreds of thousands. It is really difficult, or maybe impossible, to "reclaim" a young person who has already learned to be cynical and care only about personal gains and money in the bank.

NOTE

1. Full references to these studies are in "References to Chapter Five."

REFERENCES

Austin, James. 2000. *Zen and the Brain: Toward an Understanding of Meditation and Consciousness.* Cambridge, MA: The MIT Press.
Edwards, Mark, Jr. 2006. *Religion on Our Campuses.* New York: Palgrave.
Jackson, Phil. 1996. *Sacred Hoops: Spiritual Lessons of a Hardwood Warrior.* New York: Hyperion.
Langer, Ellen. 1997. *The Power of Mindful Learning.* Cambridge, MA: Perseus Books Group.
Marsden, George. 1994. *The Soul of the American University: From Protestant Establishment to Established Nonbelief.* Oxford: Oxford University Press.
Palmer, Parker. 1993. *To Know as We Are Known: Education as a Spiritual Journey.* New York: Harper Collins.
Pope, Loren. 2012. *Colleges that Change Lives.* New York: Penguin Books.

Bibliography

Anacker, Stefan. 1984. *Seven Works of Vasubandhu: The Buddhist Psychological Doctor*. Delhi: Motilal Banarsidas.

Arum, Richard, and Josipa Roksa. 2011. *Academically Adrift: Limited Learning on College Campuses*. Chicago: University of Chicago Press.

Astin, Alexander. 1993. *What Matters in College? Four Critical Years Revisited*. San Francisco: Jossey-Bass Publishers.

Austin, James. 2000. *Zen and the Brain; Toward an Understanding of Meditation and Consciousness*. Cambridge, MA: The MIT Press.

Batchelor, Martine. 2011. "Meditation and Mindfulness," *Contemporary Buddhism* 12.1: 157–64.

Batchelor, Steven. 1998. *Buddhism without Beliefs*. New York: Riverhead Books.

Bethel, Dayle. 1989. *Education for Creative Living: Ideas and Proposals of Tsunesaburo Makiguchi*. Ames: Iowa State University Press.

Blows, M. 1993. *Towards the Whole Person: Integrating Eastern and Western Approaches to Body-Mind Skills*. Kenthurst, NSW: Linking Publications.

Bond, George. 2004. *Buddhism at Work; Community Development, Social Empowerment, and the Sarvodaya Movement*. Bloomfield, CT: Kumarian.

Brandon, David. 1976. *Zen in the Art of Helping*. Boston: Routledge.

Brown, Richard. 2011. "The Mindful Teacher as the Foundation of Contemplative Pedagogy," in (ed.) J. Simmer-Brown, *Meditation and the Classroom*. New York: State University of New York Press.

Brown, Sid. 2008. *A Buddhist in the Classroom*. New York: State University of New York Press.

Buddhist Text Translation Society (BTTS). 1995. *In Memory of the Venerable Master Hsuan Hua*. Burlingame, CA: Buddhist Text Translation Society Press.

———. 2001. *Out of the Earth It Emerges: Wonderful Enlightenment Mountain*. Burlingame, CA: Buddhist Text Translation Society Press.

Chandler, Stuart. 2004. *Establishing a Pure Land on Earth; The Foguangshan Buddhist Perspective on Modernization and Globalization*. Honolulu: Hawaii University Press.

Chang, Otto. 2012. "Accounting Ethics Education: Comparison with Buddhist Ethics Education Framework," *Journal of Religion and Business Ethics* 3: 1–22.

Cheng, Yen. 2012. "Vegetarianism," *Tzu Chi*, winter 2012: 60–72.

Chiesa, A., and A. Seretti. 2009. "Mindfulness-Based Stress Reduction for Stress Management in Healthy People: Review and Meta-analysis," *Journal of Alternative and Complementary Medicine* 15.5: 593–600.

City of Ten Thousand Buddhas (CTTB). 2011a. "The Traditions of the City of Ten Thousand Buddhas," http://www.advite.com.

———. 2011b. "Vegetarianism," http://www.advite.com.

Coburn, Thomas. 2007a. "The Arts and the 'In-between' Spaces," *Naropa Magazine*, spring issue: 1.

———. 2007b. "Naropa University: Reflecting the Interplay of Discipline and Delight," *Bodhi Magazine*, v. 9: 126–29.

Coburn, Thomas, Fran Grace, Anne Klein et al. 2011. "Contemplative Pedagogy: Frequently Asked Questions," *Teaching Theology and Religion*, v. 14, issue 2: 167–74.

Coleman, James. 2000. *The New Buddhism: The Western Transformation of an Ancient Tradition*. New York: Oxford University Press.

Dass, Ram. 1971. *Be Here Now*. Taos, NM: Lama Foundation.

Davidson, Richard. 2002. "Toward a Biology of Positive Affect and Compassion." In (ed.) Davidson, R. and Harrington, A. *Visions of Compassion: Western Scientists and Tibetan Buddhists Examine Human Nature*. (New York: Oxford University Press): 107–31.

De Melo, Silva. 2000. "Makiguchi Project in Action – Enhancing Education for Peace," *Journal of Oriental Studies* 10: 62–93.

De Silva, Padmal. 2000. "Buddhism and Psychotherapy," *Hsi Lai Journal of Humanistic Buddhism* 1: 169–81.

DRBU. 2001. *General Catalog 2001*.

———. 2010–2012. *General Catalog 2010–2012*.

———. 2014. *Spring 2014 Semester Course Schedule: Ukiah and Berkeley Campuses*.

Edwards, Mark, Jr. 2006. *Religion on Our Campuses*. New York: Palgrave.

Epstein, Ronald. 2006. "Buddhist Resources on Vegetarianism and Animal Welfare," www.sfsu.edu.

———. 2010. "A Portrait of the Venerable Master Hsuan Hua," *Religion East and West* 10: 148–49.

———. 2014. "Resources for the Study of Buddhism," www.sfsu.edu

Fisher, Danny. 2010. "University of the West Celebrates $1.1 Million in Scholarships for Buddhist Studies," http://dannyfisher.org/2010/02/02.

Flagg, Chuck. 2011. "The City of Ten Thousand Buddhas," *Morgan Hill Times*. March 20, 2011.

Foard, James, et al. (ed.). 1996. *The Pure Land Tradition: History and Development*. Berkeley: Regents of the University of California.

Fu, Zhiying. 2008. (Tr. by Robert Smitheram). *Bright Star, Luminous Cloud: The Life of a Simple Monk*. Hacienda Heights, CA: Buddha Light Publishing.

Gamble, Adam, and Takesato Watanabe. 2004. *A Public Betrayed: An Inside Look at Japanese Media Atrocities and Their Warnings to the West*. Washington, DC: Regnery Publishing.

Gardner, Howard. 1990. *Art Education and Human Development*. Los Angeles: Getty Publications.

Goldwarg, Jill. 2003. "Revisiting," *Newsletter of Naropa University*, July:12.

Goodland, Robert, and Jeff Anhang. 2009. "Livestock and Climate Change," *World Watch*, November–December.

Habito, Ruben, and Jacqueline Stone. 1994. *Revisiting Nichiren*. Special Issue of *Japanese Journal of Religious Studies* 26, no. 304.

Haimson, Leonie. 2010. "The Benefits of Small Classes," www.classsizematters.org/benefits; retrieved on June 25, 2014.

Hayward, Jeremy. 2008. *Warrior-King of Shamabala: Remembering Chogyam Trungpa*. Boston: Wisdom Publications.

Heffron, John. 2009. "Soka Education as a Philosophy of Life: The SUA Experience," *Soka Education*, n. 2:143–48.

History of Naropa. 2013. http://www.naropa.edu/about-naropa/history.

Holtom, D. C. 1992. *The Political Philosophy of Modern Shinto*, vol. XLIX, p. 2. Tokyo: Transactions of the Asiatic Society of Japan.

Horn, Stacy. 2014. *Imperfect Harmony: Finding Happiness Singing with Others*. New York: Workman Publishing.

Hsing Yun. 2006a. *Core Teachings: Buddhist Practice and Progress*. Hacienda Heights, CA: Buddha Light Publishing.
———. 2008. *Humanistic Buddhism*. Hacienda Heights, CA: Buddha Light Publishing.
———. 2006b. *A Look at Modern Issues: Buddhism and Our Changing Society*. Hacienda Heights, CA: Buddha Light Publishing.
Hsu, Tai. 2010. "Humanistic Buddhism." Hacienda Heights, CA: Foguang Shan Hsi Lai Temple.
I.B.P.S., Buddhist Memorial Complex. 2010. *The Ultimate Care*. Hacienda Heights, CA: Buddha Light Publishing.
Ikeda, Daisaku. 1996. *A New Humanism*. New York: Weatherhil.
———. 2001. *Soka Education*. Santa Monica: Middleway Press, 2001.
Jackson, Phil. 1996. *Sacred Hoops: Spiritual Lessons of a Hardwood Warrior*. New York: Hyperion.
Jedeikin, Jenny. 2013. "5 Benefits of a Small Class Size," www.phoenix.edu; retrieved on June 26, 2014.
Johnson, Owen. 2009. "Earth Day Celebration Signals Completion of Naropa Green House." *Naropa Magazine*, spring issue: 2–3.
Kaza, Stephanie. 2005. "Western Buddhist Motivations for Vegetarianism," *Worldviews: Global Religions, Culture and Ecology* 9.3: 385–411.
Kindler, Anna. 2003. "Commentary: Visual Culture, Visual Brain, and Art Education," *Studies in Art Education*, vol. 4, n. 3: 290–96.
Kisala, Robert. 2004. "Soka Gakkai: Searching for the Mainstream," in (eds.) Lewis, James and Petersen, Jesper. *Controversial New Religions*. Oxford: Oxford University Press.
Kosareff, Jason. 2011. "University of the West Participates in Rosemead Water Recycling Project," *Buddhist News*: http://www.uwest.edu/site
Kumagai, Kazunori. 2000. "Value-Creating Pedagogy and Japanese Education in the Modern Era," *The Journal of Oriental Studies*, v. 10: 29–46.
Kwee, M. G. 1990. *Psychotherapy, Meditation and Health*. London: East-West Publications.
Langer, Ellen. 1997. *The Power of Mindful Learning*. Cambridge, MA: Perseus Books.
Lin, Irene. 2006. "Journey to the Far West: Chinese Buddhism in America," in Tanya Storch (ed.) *Religions and Missionaries in the Pacific, 1500-1900*. Aldershot, UK: Ashgate Publishing, Ltd.
Lindtner, Christian. 1982. *Nagarjuniana: Studies in the Writings and Philosophy of Nagarjuna*. Copenhagen, Denmark: Akademisk Forlag.
Lopez, Donald (ed.). 1997. *Religions of Tibet in Practice*. Princeton, NJ: Princeton University Press.
Ly, Boreth. 2012. "Buddhist Walking Meditations," *Positions* 20. 1: 267–85.
Mackenzie, Matthew. 2008. "Self-Awareness without a Self," *Asian Philosophy* vol. 18: 245–66.
Macy, Joanna. 1991. *Mutual Causality in Buddhism and General Systems Theory: The Dharma of Natural Systems*. Albany, NY: State University of New York Press.
Marsden, George. 1994. *The Soul of the American University: From Protestant Establishment to Established Nonbelief*. Oxford: Oxford University Press.
Master Xingyun. 2012. *Bells, Gongs and Wooden Fish*. Hacienda Heights, CA: Buddha Light Publishing.
———. 1999. *Humble Table, Wise Fare: Hospitality for the Heart*, translated by Tom Manzo and Dr. Shujan Cheng. Rosemead: Hsi Lai University Press.
———. 2006. *The Light of Hope*, translated by Cathie Chen. Burlingame: Buddhist Text Translation Society.
McDonald, Kathleen. 2010. *Awakening the Kind Heart: How to Meditate on Compassion*. Boston: Wisdom Publications.
McDonald, Raymond. 2013. "Second Overnight Sit Builds Diverse Sangha at UWest," *University of the West Student Government*: http://www.uwsa.net/current-business
McRae, John. 2003. *Seeing through Zen: Encounter, Transformation, and Genealogy in Chinese Chan Buddhism*. Berkeley, CA: University of California Press.

Metraux, Daniel. 1996. "The Soka Gakkai: Buddhism and the Creation of a Harmonious and Peaceful Society," In Christopher Queen and Sally King (eds.), *Engaged Buddhism: Buddhist Liberation Movements in Asia* (New York: State University of New York Press).

Midal, Fabrice. 2004. *Chogyam Trungpa: His Life and Vision*. Boston: Shamabala Publication.

Miller, Andrea. 2008. "Profile: The University of the West," *Buddhadharma: The Practitioner's Quarterly*: http://thebuddhadharma.com/issuees/2008/fall/profile

Miller, John. 2006. *Educating for Wisdom and Compassion*. Thousand Oaks, CA: Corwin Press.

Mitchell, Donald. 2013. *Buddhism: Introducing the Buddhist Experience*, 3rd Edition. New York: Oxford University Press.

Miyata, Koichi. 2000. *Ideas and Influence of Tsunesaburo Makiguchi: Special Issue of the Journal of Oriental Studies*, 10. Tokyo: The Institute of Oriental Philosophy.

Mukpo, Diana. 2006. *Dragon Thunder: My Life with Chogyam Trungpa*. Boston: Shamabala Publication.

Naropa University. 2010. *Naropa University Academic Catalog*, 2010–2011.

———. 2003. *Newsletter of Naropa University*.

Newton, Edmund. 1998. "Buddhists Concentrate Hsi Lai Temple," *Los Angeles Times*.

Paine, Jeffrey. 2004. *Re-Enchantment: Tibetan Buddhism comes to the West*, 1st Edition. New York: W. W. Norton & Company.

Palmer, Parker. 1993. *To Know as We Are Known: Education as a Spiritual Journey*. New York: Harper Collins.

Plank, Katarina. 2010. "Mindful Medicine: The Growing Trend of Mindfulness-based Therapies in the Swedish Health Care System," *Finnish Journal of Ethnicity and Migration* vol. 5: 47–55.

Pope, Loren. 2012. *Colleges that Change Lives*. New York: Penguin Books.

Powers, Douglas. "Buddhism and Postmodernism," http://www.drbu.org/content

Powers, John. 1995. *Introduction to Tibetan Buddhism*. Ithaca, NY: Snow Lion Publications.

Progrebin, Robin. 2007. "Book Tackles Old Debate: Role of Art in School." *The New York Times*, August 4, 2007.

Pulley, John. 2001. "Soka University Tries to Invent College," *The Chronicle of Higher Education* (January 2001): 18–19.

Salzberg, Sharon. 1997. *Loving Kindness: The Revolutionary Art of Happiness*. Boston: Shamabala Publications.

Sandel, Michael. 2012. *What Money Can't Buy: The Moral Limits of Markets*. New York: Farrar, Straus, and Giroux.

Selingo, Jeffrey. 2013. *College (Un)bound: The Future of Higher Education and What it Means for Students*. Boston: New Harvest.

Seppala, E., et al. 2013. "Social Connection and Compassion: Important Predictors of Health and Well-being," *Social Research* 80.3: 411–30.

Sharma, Namrata. 1999. *Value Creators in Education: Japanese Educator Makiguchi and Mahatma Gandhi and Their Relevance for the Indian Education.* New Delhi: Regency Publications.

Silberman, Steve. 2006. "Married to the Guru," *Shambala Sun*, November 2006: 1–6.

Simmer-Brown, Judith. 2009. "The Question Is the Answer: Naropa University's Contemplative Pedagogy," *Religion and Education*, summer issue.

Simmer-Brown, Judith, and Fran Grace. 2011. *Meditation and the Classroom: Contemplative Pedagogy for Religious Studies*. New York: State University of New York Press.

Soka University of America. 2012. *Undergraduate Catalog 2012–2013*.

Storch, Tanya. 2014. *The History of Chinese Buddhist Bibliography: Censorship and Transformation of the Tripitaka*. New York: Cambria Press.

———. 2000. "The Past Explains the Present: State Control Over Religious Communities in Medieval China." *The Medieval History Journal* 3, October.

Strauss, William, and Neil Howe. *Millennials Rising: The Next Great Generation*. New York: Vintage Original, 2000.

Strum, Deborah, et al. 2012. "The Elements: A Model of Mindful Supervision," *Journal of Creativity in Mental Health* 7.3: 222–32.

Thich, Nhat Hahn. 1978. *The Heart of Understanding: Commentaries on the Prajnaparamita Heart Sutra*. Berkeley, CA: Parallax Press.

Trungpa, Chogyam. 2000a. *Born in Tibet*. Boston: Shamabala Publications.

———. 2004. *The Collected Works of Chogyam Trungpa*, 8 vols. Boston: Shamabala Publications.

———. 2000b. *Journey without Goal*. Boston: Shamabala Publications.

Tsuji, Takehisa (trans.). 1979. Online collection of quotes from *Axioms of Tsunesaburo Makiguchi*, 1979 Japanese edition. http://www.tmakiguchi.org/quotes/.

United Nations Environmental Program (UNEP). 2010. *Assessing the Environmental Impacts of Consumption and Production*.

Walker, Richard. 2013. "Soka University of America's 10th Anniversary," *SGI Quarterly* (April 2013): 1–3.

Wallace, Alan. 2004. *The Four Immeasurables: Cultivating a Boundless Heart*. Ithaca, NY: Snow Lion Publications.

Wayment, Heidi, et al. 2011. "Doing and Being: Mindfulness, Health, and Quiet Ego Characteristics among Buddhist Practitioners," *Journal of Happiness Studies* 12.4: 575–89.

Williams, J., and J. Kabat-Zinn. 2011. "Mindfulness: Diverse Perspectives on Its Meaning, Origins, and Multiple Applications at the Intersection of Science and Dharma," *Contemporary Buddhism: An Interdisciplinary Journal* 12.1: 1–18.

Wilson, Jeff. 2014. *Mindful America: The Mutual Transformations of Buddhist Meditation and American Culture*. New York: Oxford University Press.

Xuan, Pan. 2013. *Buddha-Land in the Human World*. Hacienda Heights, CA: Buddha Light Publishing.

Yung, Dong. 2006. "Chinese Buddhism and Economic Progress," *Hsi Lai Journal of Humanistic Buddhism* 7: 264–78.

Index

About the Author

Tanya Storch is professor of religious studies at the University of the Pacific in California. She taught Asian religions at several universities, including the University of New Mexico, the University of Pennsylvania, and the University of Florida. She holds a PhD from the University of Pennsylvania and an MA from the University of St. Petersburg, Russia. Dr. Storch's previous publications include *Chinese Scrolls*; *Religions and Missionaries in the Pacific, 1500–1800*; *Japan under Snow*; *Mastering the Five Elements*; and *Chinese Buddhist Bibliography: Censorship and Transformation of the Tripitaka*. Overall, she has produced nearly thirty academic and artistic publications in the field of Asian religion and spirituality.